When it comes to sage financial wisdom, Ellie Kay practices what she proclaims and as such is more than qualified to advise those eager to make effective lifestyle changes with their money. Her practical "take-away" tips and knowledge coupled with rock solid biblical encouragement all but ensures lasting change for those wise enough to follow her lead.

JULIE BARHILL
Author of *She's Gonna Blow!*, *Til Debt Do Us Part*,
Radical Forgiveness

Ellie Kay has put together an incredible resource for families who are striving to do it right. She not only has loaded this book with biblical wisdom, but has included the application of that biblical wisdom in practical and very useable ways. Ellie is gifted as a communicator, and I trust that this book is going to have a long life. It is with joy and enthusiasm that I recommend *Half-Price Living*.

RON BLUE
Author of *The New Master Your Money*

Today's military families are experiencing tremendous financial pressures as they serve their nation at home and abroad. Ellie Kay's book *Half-Price Living* will be a valuable and unique tool to help those military families discover practical and creative ways to navigate these tough financial waters. Sprinkling humor and wit throughout, Ellie has provided an entertaining, timely, and practical book that will financially fortify our warriors and their spouses as they serve our nation and lead their families. Once again Ellie has delivered hope to our "Heroes at Home" with *Half-Price Living*.

MAJOR GENERAL BOB DEES, USA (Retired)
Executive Director, Military Ministry, Campus Crusade

Ellie Kay may well be "America's Family Financial Expert" but when she gives advice it's like your best friend over a cup of coffee instead of an E. F. Hutton advisor over an imposing oak desk. And she doesn't give grand theories of money management, but principles that she has implemented in her own life; you know—the stuff that really works! So if you want to laugh while you learn, let *Half-Price Living* show you how to live better than you ever thought you could on less money than you ever thought possible.

ANITA RENFROE
Comedian, Author of *If It's Not One Thing, It's Your Mother*

Ellie Kay is practical, funny, and committed to help others be good stewards of their resources. If your goal is to live on one income, *Half-Price Living* is a must-read. Based on her own experiences and insightful research, Ellie Kay shares pointers to help couples stretch their budgets and make living on one income a possibility.

JAMES AND BETTY ROBISON
LIFE Outreach International
Fort Worth, Texas

Fascinating and delightful reading as well as highly practical—this book will be gratefuly received by the readers.

H. NORMAN WRIGHT
Author of *Before You Say "I Do"*

1/2

Price Living

Secrets to Living Well on One Income

ELLIE KAY

MOODY PUBLISHERS
CHICAGO

© 2007 by
ELLIE KAY

All Scripture quotations are taken from the *New American Standard Bible,* © 1960, 1962, 1963, 1968, 1971, 1972, 1973, 1975, 1977, and 1995 The Lockman Foundation, La Habra, Calif. Used by permission.

Cover and Interior Design: www.DesignByJulia.com
Photo Image in Name: Jimi Allen
Author Family Photo: Craig Rowitz
Other Images: jupiterimages.com
Editorial Services: Julie-Allyson Ieron

ISBN: 0-8024-3432-0
ISBN-13: 978-0-8024-3432-6

Library of Congress Cataloging-in-Publication Data

Kay, Ellie.
    Half-price living : secrets to living well on one income / by Ellie Kay.
        p. cm.
    Includes bibliographical references.
    ISBN-13: 978-0-8024-3432-6
        1. Finance, Personal—Religious aspects. 2. Consumer education.
    3. Home economics—Accounting. I. Title.

HG179.K3788 2007
332.024—dc22

                                                            2006029581

We hope you enjoy this book from Moody Publishers. Our goal is to provide high-quality, thought-provoking books and products that connect truth to your real needs and challenges. For more information on other books and products written and produced from a biblical perspective, go to www.moodypublishers.com or write to:

Moody Publishers
820 N. LaSalle Boulevard
Chicago, IL 60610

1 3 5 7 9 10 8 6 4 2

Printed in the United States of America

If I could choose a sister, I'd choose a friend so true
If I could choose a neighbor, I know that I'd choose you
If I could pick a person to post guard at my back
I'd chose a warrior faithful, whose character does not lack
If I could choose a dreamer, who listened away the day
I'd choose my kindred spirit, who helped me find my way
You are a sister faithful, You are the friend so true
You are a dreaming spirit, and, Wendy, I pick you.

Half-Price Living is dedicated
to my friend and business manager,
Wendy Wendler

CONTENTS

ACKNOWLEDGMENTS

When I was a girl, my favorite Golden Book story was *The Little Red Hen.* One day Little Red Hen found a grain of wheat that she thought should be planted. None of her fellow farm dwellers was willing to plant it. So, she planted it; later, with her chicks she tended and harvested it. When it came time to eat, she and her chicks ate the bounty. She found, however, that although the duck, cat, and dog were unwilling to work with the seed, they were willing to eat it. But, by then it was too late.

All the books I've written over the years have been a collective labor of family and friends—those who truly believe in the work. Friends have come and gone. Business associates have drifted in and out again. But some diehards remain.

I want to acknowledge those people who have contributed to my professional life over the long haul. This, of course, must start with my husband and children. Bob, a.k.a. "Beloved," has been there through planting, harvesting, and threshing seasons. For some reason, it seems the harvest is a lot easier than the threshing! Thank you for your diligence, strength, and courage in the field. Daniel, Philip, Bethany, Jonathan, and Joshua have allowed me to write the good, bad, and ugly of their lives in exchange for hugs and kisses, chocolate chip cookies, and season passes to Six Flags Magic Mountain. This fresh-baked bread would taste like straw in my mouth if you chickies were not here to enjoy it with us. I love you so.

Steve Laube, my former editor and current agent, is a constant in the ever-changing world of publishing. He planted the first writing seed by pulling that proposal out of the weeds and into a printing press. He is wise and generous with his authors and friends. Wendy Wendler was there as a personal assistant and speaking team member when those first few seeds were taking root. She's been a worker in the field that has grown dramatically. She came in early and stayed late; we've faced more than a few threshings together. Now, as my business manager she is with me in harvesting old fields and planting new ones. Brenda Taylor is a friend who has brought me out to almost every town her military family has lived in during the last decade. She promotes me professionally at every turn and lets me write all manner of stories about her. Thank you, Brenda, for your friendship and consistency. Madeline is my prophet-sister-friend who speaks with amazing power. I would say she's fertilizer on the field, but that would be fairly cruddy of me. Thank you, Madeline, for writing the vision in my heart and in stone. Cheryl Shelton is a weather vane, pointing me in the right direction and warning of impending weather that could impact the field. Thank you for letting me know which way the wind is blowing.

I was once a tenant farmer in Peg Short's field years ago. She was my current acquiring editor whose enthusiasm never waned even when deadlines were moved and contracts were delayed. I thank you for your desire to work together and look forward to a long and prosperous harvest with my friends at Moody.

While other friends and family have enriched my life in immeasurable ways, these faithful friends have enriched my fields over the course of many years. We've planted, tilled, harvested, crushed, and baked the bread together. Let's forget the carbs and dig into eat that bread with guilt-free joy—and while we're living recklessly, let's throw in a Frappuccino too!

. . . learning to live on one income is a little like adopting a new puppy.

89%
factor

WHY LIVE on One Income?

I have five children, two stepchildren, and this year, much to our delight, we got a new baby. We named the cute little guy, "Buddy." He doodles all the time, sleeps slightly more than he doodles, and eats anything he can find—including several strategically stashed hoards of PMS chocolate.

Buddy is a dog.

He's graduating this Saturday at the top of his obedience school class. He's going to participate in a ceremony and our whole family will be there. He's getting the valedictorian and perfect-attendance awards. He loves to give kisses and can shake hands upon request. After he's groomed he sashays with a prance that says, "Hey, look at me! I'm handsome!" He loves his daily walks and enjoys going "bye-bye" in the car.

I love that dog.

On the other hand, we discovered that if we don't place a chew toy in every room in the house, he will create his own. Yesterday, he chewed the gorgeous white pearl and satin wedding album from my stepdaughter's big day. The week before, he chewed my sentimental handmade Adirondack basket (crafted by a woman who later died of cancer) that had been given to me as a farewell/moving gift from the ladies of Fort Drum, New York. Before that, he chewed my new designer pumps. I now get compliments on their "interesting pattern of indentations." He also discovered when the backyard sprinklers go off it makes mud in the flower beds, and he decided to roll in the mess and become a muddy Buddy.

I don't like that dog.

Learning to live on one income is a little like adopting a new puppy. It's a commitment; it's harder than you think; and it's rewarding and fulfilling. I know the analogy sounds simplistic, because the children we affect by staying home have eternal souls—whereas, a dog needs to live it up in the here and now. Contributing to our kids' future is a tad more important than making sure the puppy gets outside before he embarrasses himself. But I said it was a "little like" adopting a puppy—not *exactly* like it. Both of these situations are ones you both love and dislike—sometimes at the same time. But if having a Buddy is like deciding to live on one income, it becomes optional—a choice. You don't have to have a puppy. You don't have to live on one income. But if you *do* decide to live on one income, this resource will help you do it well.

This book is written to 89 percent of working moms. These are the women who answered a January 2006 www.clubmom.com survey and said, "If I could afford to stay home with my kids, I would." I'm *not* interested in entering the "Mommy Wars" debate about whether a mom should have a career inside or outside of the home. I *am* interested in helping moms who *want* to make the transition to one income learn how to cut costs in half and have double the fun in the process.

Half-Price Living means you can have half the stress, because you're not balancing work and home. Living on one income means you can have half the clutter in your home, because you can take the time to simplify your life. Living on one income means you have the time to cook instead of grabbing fast food, and thereby have half the health risks in your life. It can also mean you have time to comparison shop, learn the fine art of saving money, and cut some bills in half.

In the first few years of my marriage to "The World's Greatest Fighter Pilot" (my hubby, Bob), we decided to adopt a *half-price living* lifestyle. I would stay home with the babies. We had a cross-stitch on the wall that said, "Blessed are the poor, for they be us." Those early years were filled with self-fulfilling nursery rhymes. There were "Old Mother Hubbard" times when we didn't have extra food in the cupboards. I felt like the "Old Lady in the Shoe" with so many kids I didn't know what to do. We were afraid "Humpty Dumpty" would fall off the financial wall and everything would come tumbling down.

What I learned was this: *half-price living* can be achieved. Even if you have a huge debt load (we had $40,000 of consumer debt with nothing to show for our trouble), it can be done. Even if you take a pay cut (Bob took a $15,000 per year pay cut to go into the military), it can be done. Even if you love your job (hello? I was a small biz owner from the age of five), it can be done. Even if you need a job, you can have a whole new career come out of this decision. And even if you have no faith (I honestly didn't know how we would make ends meet), it can be done.

I found out a penny saved is more than a penny earned. If I saved $10,000 a year on household goods, transportation, clothing, food, and other bills, that was the equivalent of earning $15,800 on the economy—by the time state and federal taxes were paid. So, instead of becoming a master entrepreneur, I became a master at saving money.

And it was fun.

And we didn't have to feed the family garbanzo beans every day.

And we didn't have to feel deprived.

And we didn't have to wear holey underwear.

And we had a half-price life.

And we lived well.

And we got a dog.

And he's eating my first-edition copy of *To Kill A Mockingbird*.

And I gotta go now.

I *really* don't like that dog.

******

Every Mom Is a Working Mom

I've worked outside the home and inside the home and around the home and over the home (while skydiving) and under the home (cleaning out a basement), and I'm here to say that every mom is a working mom—whether you are in the workforce or you stay at home. According to the U.S. Census Bureau, the United States had an estimated 5.5 million stay-at-home parents in 2005; 5.4 million of those were moms.[1] Beth Brykman writes, "As mothers, we sometimes feel as though we're judged by other mothers for life choices we've made, specifically it's the stay-at-home moms vs. career moms."[2]

Have you felt left out or lost friends over your choices? Situations like this probably occur between moms more often than we realize, but can both groups find a happy medium and support each other in life?

Suzie is a team leader in a software company in New York. She stayed at home as a home-based consultant for fifteen years but found herself back in the workforce outside the home due to a family move and her husband's career change. "I've been a stay-at-home mom and a working mom, and I think there is a mistaken belief that the other side has it all when both sides have pluses and minuses. While employed mothers earn income and have the social status that comes with working outside the home, they also have a lot of guilt about not spending enough time with their children. A stay-at-home mother can't begin to imagine how much guilt working mothers have unless she has worked outside the home as a mother herself."

Dawn, a former Air Force officer and engineer from California, is now home full time with her three sons. "In all honesty, I do miss the structure of the workday, having challenges to overcome, and working with adults. Our lives are much less hectic than if I worked; we have a well-kept home, healthy meals, and time for family fun. My husband is less stressed since I can take care of many household things during the day that he would have to take care of if I worked." But Dawn doesn't always get a rosy reception from other moms.

She's been around women who define themselves by their job description and when they hear Dawn belongs to a one-income family, their reactions can be harsh. "I've had some of these women immediately turn on their well-heeled feet and find another woman to talk [with]—one with a more current résumé."

CEO Mom: Past, Present, and Future

As a little girl, I was nicknamed "Moneybags" by my dad. I drove my parents wild with my ability to make money and refusal to spend it. Not only did I run a future corporation out of my second-grade locker, but I saved most of the earnings. Business was my childhood passion, and selling came as naturally as running barefoot in summer grass. As a seven-year-old, I sold buzzer handshakes from a wind-up toy in a box of cereal. As an eight-year-old, I sold all my Spanish grandma's eggplant door to door (I *loathe* eggplant!). By the time I was in fourth grade, I was selling candy bars that I bought wholesale and marked up at a 40 percent profit margin. To this day, little "Moneybags" remembers counting all the shiny nickels, dimes, and quarters. I felt I was rich.

By the time high school rolled around, I'd mastered a half-dozen home businesses, and my entrepreneurial spirit was well developed. I paid cash for a trip to Spain at age twelve and also paid cash for my first car at fifteen. I dreamed of becoming a CEO for a major corporation in an effort to "be" somebody. During college I worked for a broker and loved it. I eventually worked full time for this firm and managed to almost double their number of policies by developing marketing strategies to generate new business. I was on my way to becoming somebody (at least in my eyes)—only this time I was counting tens, twenties, and fifties. I felt God had given me the ability to make money because I also had the gift of giving back out of my earnings.

Then I met a handsome fighter pilot, we got married, and I learned a new definition of what it means to "be" somebody. It seems I was to be pregnant for seven years. The babies rolled down the delivery ramp . . . over and over and over again until we were supporting seven kiddos. Two of those precious children were my stepdaughters and five were my own. Suddenly, the idea of climbing the corporate ladder to fulfill a young woman's idea of success wasn't nearly as significant as being "somebody" to our children.

When you consider the fact that we were to take the show on the road with the Air Force and move eleven times in thirteen years, it's evident that my dreams needed to shift for a season.

It was hard to follow the CEO phantom while following my daring young man around the world. So the dream of staying home with priceless children became my new reality. I loved my babies—and wouldn't have traded any one of them. However, there were days when they drove me *berzerko*—days when they played mischief wars and tried to redecorate the kitchen cabinets with chocolate syrup and miniature marshmallows. On *those* days I would have traded *all* of them for a pair of panty hose, a sensible suit, and a nine-to-five job with a coffee break (with Starbucks java and decadent Godiva chocolate).

Even though I loved the challenge and fulfillment in the business world, I loved the priceless moments and eternal milestones shared with my babies more. The challenge of *half-price living* was one both Bob and I were eager to try. The fact that Mr. Fighter Pilot Dude was supportive of my desire to live on one income made all the difference.

Fast-forward a dozen years, and this experience of learning to live on one income became a hobby for me and then a business. I began to give seminars on saving money, wrote a book, did some TV and radio, then wrote another book. I didn't become a CEO of a major corporation; I became CEO of Ellie Kay and Company, LLC. In the process, I found that the dreams God dreams for us are better than the dreams we dream for ourselves. The key is to do what's best for your family in your situation and in your timing.

I've come to a dramatic conclusion: I can only decide what is best for my family. I don't want to pretend to know what's best for any other mom (even my best girlfriends), because judging another woman's work-or-stay-home decision can be messier than trying to snag my new water hose from Buddy's mouth after he's rolled in the mud.

A Plethora of Moms

Every mom has her own story, and we can learn a lot by reading from the experiences of others who blazed the same trail we're sojourning. I find myself inspired by reading the can-do comments that come through our offices, while other mail makes me more cautious when navigating certain paths. Still other letters are so poignant they make me blink rapidly and dab at my eyes.

What's *your* story? Will it inspire, caution, or profoundly touch another mom's life? Here are some real stories from real women.

Premier Designs for Staying at Home
Brenda from San Antonio

Brenda was a flight attendant when she lived as a military spouse in Guam and then went to school to become a teacher. She says, "I loved my job and my students, even though it was a lot of work and a huge time commitment. Staying at home can leave a woman with feelings of low self-esteem when confronted by those in the work world. I was concerned that when I stayed home with my first child we'd have less money available. We were concerned about being able to afford it." Brenda decided to start a home business and become a jeweler for the mom-friendly company, Premier Designs. This averages her about $200 each night she works and more on a monthly basis from the women she sponsors. Brenda and her husband make a point of using this cottage industry income for extras and continue to live on one primary income. This also helps prepare the household for her husband's military retirement when they may see a temporary decrease in income. She is quick to add, "My work isn't me. I know who I am as a wife, mom, and person, and where I fit into God's world."

A Zoomie Comes Home
Melissa from Texas

Melissa was from a family of high achievers. Her sister was Miss America, and Melissa graduated at the top of her class at the United States Air Force Academy. She excelled as a logistics/supply officer. Graduates of USAFA are often called "zoomies" because their careers are known to zoom to the top. Her primary concern about living on one income was "how we would meet our basic needs including health care [health insurance], house payments, food costs, and clothing allowances." She admits there are times she feels isolated at home but she makes a point of "trying to stay connected through preschool programs, Moms-in-Touch groups, PTA, church, and other community organizations."

For those who want to live on one income, Melissa has the following advice: "prioritize your 'needs' and then 'desires/wants.' Once the budget is established, try to stick to it recognizing that you may have to eliminate some materialistic things in order to be available to your loved ones. In all likelihood, they would rather have you, your time, and attention more than the things you can buy them anyway. If you are going to transition from two incomes to one, then take a part-time job and downsize slowly until you are able to live off one income."

Author and Speaker Starts from Home
Pam Farrel from San Diego

Pam is the best-selling author of too many books to count, including *Red-Hot Monogomy*. She and her husband, Bill, had the conviction that one of the parents should raise the kids, so they made a vow to each other to have one of them home full time until the kids got to school. After that, they shared parenting roles so that even after the kids were in school their family would get top priority. She said those lean years were much simpler. They enjoyed one checkbook and simple pleasures such as dinners at home, walks in the park, and sitting by the fireplace.

"We were in school, seminary, and then in youth ministry, so our one salary was never high. But the people and parents were so loving that all our needs were always met. I have prayed for milk, diapers, baby food, tennis shoes for the kids, hand-me-downs, gas, the electric bill, mortgage payments, etc. That first decade of marriage was something else!"

You don't have to be in full-time ministry to be able to have a vibrant faith while living on one income. Pam asserts, "Money was tight, but God built my faith in Him and His ability to provide; He also built my love to serve people in the local church, because I kept seeing the upside of people as they are so sweet and giving. Years later, when we were doing pretty well financially, my husband became ill. He was off work for most of two years, and we had two kids in college. Those were lean times again, but because I had all that great training from God, I knew our salary would somehow be stretched to cover all our needs, just like the oil that didn't run out for the widow and her son in the Old Testament. I have seen the goodness and faithfulness of God over and over again. In one of my books I write about the need to keep a 'Miracle Scrapbook' [where] you can keep track of answers to prayers so that, when your needs get bigger, you can be reminded your God has not gotten smaller—He will and does provide."

An Income Called "Saving"
Shannon from Oklahoma

Shannon was visiting her sister in Oklahoma when my team gave a live event and she bought some of my books. She says, "I got so excited about saving money that I reread them and highlighted certain areas. Within the first month, I cut my grocery bills in half, learned how to find quality clothing for less, and had my first garage sale with [your] step-by-step tips. (I made $800 from *junk*.) I was so successful that my husband and I decided I could quit my part-time job as a receptionist." Shannon concludes, "My children [she has three] are now contributing to us living on one paycheck and learning about money management while helping the family."

Single Mom, a Single Income
Dana from Denver

Dana wrote me an amazing letter: "I'm a single mom who desperately wanted to stay at home with my two-year-old girl, but I have limited financial resources. I tried your methods to cut costs and even found a way to get extra coupon inserts (from the recycling center at our apartment complex). Now I get a dozen copies of the coupon inserts from the Sunday paper, and I'm getting *dozens* of *free* items each week. Last week, I took eight bags of toiletries to a crisis pregnancy center. Here, I thought I was the needy one, and you showed me through your helpful instruction that I can be the one to *give* help." Dana wrote again, some months later and said she had a greater sense of self-esteem and worth as she learned to manage on her limited income and still reach out to help others. She concludes, "This has been life-changing for me, and I can stay home with my two-year-old daughter!"

A China Doll for Linda

Ward and Linda from England call their daughter Kara (adopted from China) a gift from God. Linda says, "It was our plan from the beginning for me to stay home with our child. The years go by too fast for me to miss even one of them. Also, we planned to homeschool, which required me being home."

It was soon evident that this beautiful little girl with dark hair and porcelain-like skin had a special gift for writing. The fact that Linda was home to encourage and nurture the gift provided her daughter with the soil she needed to blossom in the area, of the written word. But this family has not been without its share of heartache. Recently, Kara started experiencing pain in her arm, and a large bone cyst was discovered. The family went through several steps and doctors before they got the devastating diagnosis: cancer.

Linda explains: "Osteosarcoma is a deadly bone cancer. It takes intensive chemo (at least eighteen weeks of inpatient chemo, and probably several weeks for complications) and a major surgery to give her a chance."

This family is in the middle of their fight as Kara continues treatments after having her tumor removed and her bone replaced with a metal rod. You can go to www.karasiert.com to read some of Kara's stories and link to her cancer Web site (or you can e-mail me for an update).

Linda has the satisfaction of knowing her decision to stay home with Kara from the time they adopted her has been one of the best things she has ever done. She has treasured *every* moment. Linda has also nurtured Kara's dream of seeing her work published.

I'd like to share a story Kara wrote just after her eighth birthday. Allow me to help Kara realize a dream of seeing her first story in print as I share this space with her wisdom, wit, and work.

A "Real" Dog's Story by Kara Siert, age 8

It was a beautiful, bright, sunny day. But I, the poodle without a name, sitting in a pile of toys, felt miserable. My sisters felt the same way I did. I didn't have any brothers, just sisters. I had been living in the attic for as long as I remembered. I don't know how I got here, but I do remember being bought from a toy store. After that, I don't remember anything at all. Now, I spend my life in a dusty, dull attic.

Just then, the door to the attic opened. A lady entered. She turned on the light, so I could see her clearly. The light to the attic hadn't been turned on for as long as I could remember. But, it still worked.

The lady had shoulder-length blonde hair. She had on a sparkling ring, which I think is most likely her wedding ring, and a bright yellow shirt with jeans.

The light was so bright, I had to look away. I hadn't seen light for a long, long time, the last time being in the toy store, but that was so long ago.

To my surprise the lady picked up my four sisters and me and set us in the middle of the attic floor. She picked up a box of Beanie Babies and a big elephant. Then, she took us all down the ladder and into the house.

The house where she lived was tidy and clean. I didn't see a single layer of dust. In the attic, it was dusty. I hoped some kind child would come out and play with us. We might have a fancy pink little doghouse and a treat to eat. In the attic, I only ate stale dog food and hadn't tasted a treat for years. But, no one came out to play with us. Instead, the lady piled us in the corner and left.

What would happen to us? I asked myself. *Are we going to go back into that dark attic filled with dust?*

The next day, we were taken out of the house and set on a table in the driveway. The lady put a sticker that said "four dollars" on my tag, which had never been taken off. Books, games, clothes, action figures, and more animals were put onto tables and marked with prices. I looked across the street and noticed that they were putting up tables too. They were selling animals and a whole bunch of doll stuff. I glanced up the street. People were selling all kinds of toys there too. In fact, almost every house on the block was selling things.

Soon, the lady sat down on a chair behind one of the tables. People started coming and buying things.

"Oooh, look, Mommy!" exclaimed a little girl who looked like she was six. "Poodles!"

The mother and child walked over to me and my sisters.

"Stuffed poodles are four dollars," said the lady who was selling me.

Stuffed. People always called us stuffed. And we aren't. We're *real* dogs.

But the little girl saw the big elephant and they bought him instead.

The sun beat down on us, and we grew rather hot. But it was worth it if I could find someone who would take care of me and love me. I must have been sitting there for at least an hour, watching other things get bought, but my sisters and I were not included. No one had bought us yet, not yet.

Finally, a little girl and her mother came up to us! "Mom, I want one of those!" she exclaimed.

"All right, honey," the girl's mother said. "Pick one."

One! Only one? I might not get picked! I looked up at the child. But she must not have seen me, because she chose one of my sisters. I was disappointed. I might have gotten picked! I was partly glad for my sister, *partly*. But I was sort of jealous. My sister was going to get a name and someone who would love her and take care of her! And I wouldn't. I'd probably get put back into the dreary old attic.

About an hour passed. I looked over at my sisters. There

were only three of us left! But soon, one of my other sisters got bought and carried away by an excited little girl.

Then, my last sister got bought and I waved my paw at her to say good-bye.

I looked around at all my other friends. *None of them were there!* They had gotten bought too. I only saw a few games, a box of balls, a box of Beanie Babies, and some other toys, which I didn't know.

I laid my head on my paw and sadly looked across the street where other toys and animals were going to nice homes. Suddenly, I felt childish arms around me, squeezing me tight. I looked up to see a smiling girl, who had waist-length black hair, brown eyes, a pink shirt on with shorts, and tennis shoes with pink socks. Her face was shining with delight, and she squeezed me tighter and tighter until I couldn't breathe! She looked as if she was about eight.

"Mommy, Mommy!" she exclaimed. "I want this one! She's so squeezable!" The little girl hugged me tighter as her mother came closer to get a better look at me.

"Poodles are four dollars," said my owner, who was sitting behind a card table taking people's money.

"Okay, honey," said the girl's mother, "might as well."

And so I was bought by a girl named Molly and lived happily ever after.

No Guarantees, No Regrets

Kara's situation calls to the mom in me as a reminder that there are no guarantees of tomorrow. I'm thankful all my children are healthy, and I wonder what I would do if one of my babies got as sick as sweet little Kara. It reminds me there are no guarantees in our journey.

Life is always precious.

Life is sometimes short.

Life is occasionally painful.

So in the here and now, it's important we make peace with the decision to stay at home or to work outside the home. Kara's mom,

Linda, has no regrets about her decision to stay home with her daughter. To savor every delicious minute. To cherish every eternal smile. That is something she will always have. No matter what tomorrow brings.

Ten Advantages to Living on One Income

We'll conclude each chapter with tips that are practical and easy enough to implement. Some of these sections will cause you to feel good about your choices and make you want to sit down with a cup of coffee and read a Jane Austen novel. Others will make you want to grab a Power Bar and Red Bull energy drink, find the adventure, and conquer it.

So, here are ten (of the many) advantages of living on one income, as listed by ten moms who have lived the choice:

1. Less stress because you don't have to worry about balancing work and kids. *Bonnie from Ohio*

2. We can eat at home more often than when I had outside jobs. This builds a sense of family and togetherness. *Karen from California*

3. I don't have to worry about who will take care of my child if she's sick. *Linda from England*

4. I can drive for field trips and get to know my children's friends. I can also go grocery shopping during the day, and it doesn't cut into family time. *Robin from New Mexico*

5. Marriage can become stronger because you have to pull together. *Cindy from Georgia*

6. Creativity abounds as you research new, different, and fun ways to stretch one income. *Pam from California*

7. You won't miss your baby's first step, first tooth, first words, first birthday, and first, "I wuv you, Mama!" *Diane from Colorado*

8. You have more time at home to develop other passions, such as writing or speaking or exercising. *Dena from Texas*

9. You have no regrets when your kids are grown. *Gracie from Texas*

10. You have the option of being home to homeschool if you want to. *Audrey from California*

daycare center teacher, van driver, housekeeper, cook, ceo, nurse, general maintenance worker,

WORKING GIRL vs. Girlie Mom

The boardwalk was crowded on a balmy July day, and I, clad in a light blue business suit, was enjoying a genuine Coney hot dog with lots of mustard and a Diet Coke. I looked out at the landmarks along the Jersey shore and read the historical signs with interest. The sounds and smells of the boardwalk amusement park were a welcome respite from a long day of taping an episode of "Simplify Your Life," a reality show in which I was a financial expert sent in to help solve a family problem. Right now, I didn't want to help people with their problems; yet I still had a couple more hours of interviews to go after this break. The soft, cool breeze coming off the ocean was delightful. There was a sense of contagious fun in the air.

The smell of cotton candy wafted my way, and I was tempted to indulge in the sticky sweetness after the hot dog, when suddenly, an object flying overhead caught my eye. This was followed by an ear-piercing scream. Looking up, I saw a shrieking teenaged guy flying 200 feet in the air with nothing to keep him from smashing into the concrete pavement but a harness and a thin bungee cord.

A woman next to me remarked, "That boy has to be crazy! Who

in their right mind would take a ride like that on a New Jersey boardwalk? How can that be safe? He must be a few fries short of a Happy Meal." I cut my eyes to the matronly woman at my side, who was chomping on a warm pretzel.

"I don't know. It looks like fun to me. I know my kids would love it!" I added wistfully.

She took another bite of her pretzel and shook her head, mesmerized by the flying boy as I inched away from her toward a sign that read, Bungee Flying, $30. I plopped some bills on the counter at the ticket booth and asked,

"Can you go on this ride with heels or do I need tennis shoes?"

The middle-aged man in the booth warily eyed my tailored suit and blingy, strappy sandals. He responded with plenty of New Jersey attitude. "Lady, your feet won't touch de ground until you get off of the ride, so *youse* could wear those things *youse* call shoes."

He shot me a *"you're-kinda-strange-but-I've-seen-stranger"* look. "It's like this, lady, I gotta be honest with ya'; we don't have too many people in business suits bungee jumping." He shrugged. "But *whatevah* floats your boat."

The pretzel woman walked up to me. "You're not thinking of doing that, are you? Didn't you say you're a *mom*, for goodness' sake?" She must have felt it was her duty to talk me out of a moment of passionate folly. "I mean, you're not some guy; you're a girl."

I met her gaze squarely. "I am *not* a girlie mom!"

I got in the harness, and they hoisted me to the top of the 200-foot freefall area. My newfound acquaintance was gawking with open-mouthed wonder, as were many in the gathering crowd. I shouted down at them, "If anything happens to me, tell everyone I died with my suit on!"

When I got to the top, they gave the signal, and I pulled the rip cord, plunging into an adrenaline junkie's dreamworld.

"Whee!" I shouted as I whizzed over everyone's head. "Whee!!"

****

After that adventure, I went to finish the other adventure of taping the reality series episode. Ben and Suzie were blending a "yours, mine, and ours" situation, and they were expecting their first child together. Suzie wanted to stay home with the children, and while Ben thought it was a good idea, he was afraid they couldn't make ends meet. He didn't think they could pay the bills without her part-time retail job. We cranked the numbers on the Working Mom Worksheet, and right there in front of scads of TV viewers, Ben realized that after all the expenses, Suzie was making little more than 50 cents a day! His mouth dropped in disbelief as he tried to understand that all the rushed meals, all the tag-team events, all the extra hours away from home, and all the additional stress of two people working and managing kids was only yielding their family two bits an hour. I went on to show them ways to save those two bits (and more), and they've been living happily ever after on only one income. (Well, at least until the end of the series.)

Whose Decision Is It?

Sometimes it's the wife who thinks the family can't make it on one income. And sometimes it is the husband who is reluctant to support the idea of taking the plunge and live on one income. It's no wonder, is it? It can be a frightening step to realize all the responsibility for living expenses will fall on one person's shoulders. Some of the questions husbands and wives ask include: Will we have enough money? Is this the right thing for our family?

Delilah works full time as an office clerk for a paint store. She writes, "I've wanted to stay home with our son ever since he was born. My husband won't support that idea even though we've cranked the numbers and found we could do it—but barely. He wants the additional safety net of my paycheck. We drive a new van with all the luxury options, he upgrades his professional-quality bicycle every year (it's his hobby), and we just bought a big-screen TV. My son is now seven years old, and I look at these 'things' we own as something I would gladly trade in order to have more time with him at home." Delilah would love to be at home, but without her husband's willingness to sacrifice the finer things in life, she'll never make it. She concludes, "I feel like I'm working to keep us in grown-up toys!"

I'm not trying to stir things up in your house or suggest you need a marriage counselor. Hardly! But the decision to stay at home needs to be a mutual one. There needs to be support on both sides to find success and fulfillment living on one income. But it doesn't have to be scary. Many spouses at home have learned to stretch the value of a dollar; others have home businesses that supplement the one income; still others have become masters at making money in creative ways.

Stay-at-Home Compensation

A one-income family finds that the partner whose primary work is within the home, including care for the children, receives a different kind of compensation than work outside the home. Compensation can't be measured in dollars and cents exclusively. One woman may stay home because of the satisfaction of influencing her children. She doesn't want a childcare provider to see those first steps and hear the first word. She has a *choice*, and her decision is to stay home.

Other women work outside the home for a similar reason, so they can find the satisfaction of a career. They may still be paying off an expensive education or other professional fees. They may feel their destiny lies in the workplace. They, too, have a choice.

Then there's the last group, our "89-percent factor." These are women who want to stay at home, but feel they do not have a financial choice. It is important to provide facts and tips that will help working moms see what their choices *really* are. This can help them make their decisions from a financial perspective. It's up to each family to decide where mom will center her work activities— inside or outside the home.

The Suzie Show

Let's go back to our reality show couple and look a little more closely by putting ourselves in Suzie's shoes. How would you like to do the work around the house, the volunteer activities in the community and school, *and* work outside the home? Maybe some of you already have this lifestyle. Now, how would you like to do all of this for *no compensation?* This is not about volunteer work. No one expects a financial return for that kind of work—that's why it's called *volunteering.* I'm talking about the other work you do— outside the home. Why would anyone work that hard for so little compensation? Well, that's exactly what Suzie was doing—and she didn't even know it.

Suzie felt she needed to work outside the home. Ben believed the family couldn't make ends meet without her financial contribution. Suzie made an average wage of $7.50 per hour and felt she contributed to the family's finances. She had one child in day care, traveled a short distance to work, and paid no one for after-school care because she was home by the time the other children returned from school. Then Suzie, Ben, and I crunched the numbers in front of those watching on national TV. She completed the Working Mom Worksheet (on page 35) and was shocked.

The amazing fact Suzie and Ben discovered was that by working full time, *she was only making $17 per month!* They didn't realize how those extra pizza nights (because she was too tired to cook), trips to the beauty salon (to maintain a professional hairstyle), wardrobe upgrades (to look presentable in her job), and all those lunches away from home added up.

A previous client, Katie, found herself in the same situation. Katie wasn't ready to take the plunge and stay at home; she enjoyed her work and still felt it was helping her family. She realized she needed to make dramatic adjustments because she felt she wasn't keeping a lot of her paycheck. So she started carrying her lunch to work and cut back on trips to the beauty shop. Katie found this didn't benefit her much. The sacrifices allowed her to make $40 a week. Wasn't her exertion and sacrifice (and thirty hours a week away from home) worth more than $40? She decided that not only was she *not* helping her family, she wasn't helping herself, because there was a better use of her time and energy. She quit her job outside the home, and they lived on one income. This gave her the freedom to develop another business she'd always enjoyed—

cake decorating. She could do this from home. After crunching the Working Mom Worksheet a second time, she found the figures indicated that by baking ten cakes a month, she could net $350 per month.

But Katie didn't stop there. She implemented some of the ideas found in this book and is financially ahead of her peers. She has less stress in her life and the freedom to contribute to her family's financial needs by saving money in the home. (Remember, a penny saved is more than a penny earned.) Katie discovered the joy of sharing with those in need. She also contributes her time and groceries to an eternal investment—people's lives.

Crunch the Numbers

Once you come up with a figure, ask the big question. Is my time, energy and effort worth _____ dollars a week? You'll be surprised at how painless it is to cut back and save your family a significant amount of money. It's not magic; it requires work and dedication. After all, not all compensation is measured in dollars and cents. Take some time now to crunch your numbers using the worksheet on the next page.

Other assessment tools are also available as you determine the net usable income from the second paycheck. There's nothing wrong with a second opinion. I've found two excellent resources that include different variables. First, go to www.crown.org, click on the "tools" section, and find the "how much does mom really make" interactive tool. To find the "Second Income Calculator," go to moneycentral.msn.com/investor/calcs/n_spwk/main.asp. Be prepared to enter your tax filing status, income levels, taxes, and work expenses, as well as answer questions on lifestyle. They will give you the results and a summary.

The Stay-at-Home Mama

Gracie from Texas is now on the other end of the stay-at-home season of life. She says, "After all our children are grown and we are nearing retirement, I don't have any regrets about living our

Working Mom WORKSHEET™

Mom's Monthly:

Gross Income: .... _____

Taxes: .... _____

Net Spendable Income: .... _____

Extra Job Expenses:

Childcare: .... _____

Work Clothing: .... _____

Transportation/Parking: .... _____

Extra Food (*lunches purchased at work*):........... _____

Dining Out (*rather than cooking at home*): .... _____

Miscellaneous (*at-work expenses*): .... _____

Other Expenses (*that could
be avoided by working at home*): .... _____

Total Expenses: .... _____
(*for working outside the home*)

Net Monthly Income: .... _____
(*Contribution from a mom to work
outside the home*)

**Total Contribution of Mom
Working Outside the Home:** .... _____

By Ellie Kay © 2006, "America's Family Financial Expert" ™ (Figure 2.1) lives as a one-income family. It has been possible for us to live a good life without much sacrifice, having a lot of fun, enjoying each other. One of the benefits is: as a mom I wasn't exhausted in the evenings like I would have been after putting in eight or ten hours in an office. I had energy to get involved in all sorts of activities with our children and be supportive of my husband when he came home after a frazzled day of work."

Cost of Being a SAHM: Stay-at-Home Mom

M.P. Dunleavey, a writer for www.moneycentral.com wrote tongue-in-cheek, "When I was at college in the '80s (and a feisty, liberal-arts women's college it was), the notion of staying home with your kids was, shall we say, unpopular. Why spend four expensive years preparing for your supposedly brilliant career if you weren't going to put the kids where . . . feminism intended them: in daycare?"[1]

The pendulum has swung the other way since the '80s as women face the reality of trying to balance work with family and discover incredible frustration and challenge along the way. In *The Second Shift* Arlie Hochschild reported that many of the women who worked full time still did the majority of the housework.[2] Others, as we've mentioned earlier, find themselves working to pay for childcare. It seems the Supermom idea is a myth, and many women are giving up trying.

Recently I was on Fox News to discuss the fact that for Mother's Day, www.salary.com prepared a formula for calculating the commercial worth of a SAHM (stay-at-home mom). If a typical mom were paid for her momly duties, her base salary would be $43,461. Since a mother's work is never done, overtime would be an additional $88,009 for a total of $131,471 for a one-hundred-hour workweek, including six fifteen-hour days and one ten-hour day. Job titles, responsibilities, and qualifications were considered and weighed on a scale of importance, frequency, and average time spent on tasks per day. The SAHM median salary assumes the mother has at least two children of school age.[3]

After a survey of moms, www.salary.com found the following to be the best-suited job titles for SAHM, ranked from the most time-consuming to the least time-consuming:

1. daycare center teacher

2. van driver

3. housekeeper

4. cook

5. CEO

6. nurse

7. general maintenance worker

For most moms it's hard to begin to quantify what they do for their families—it's hard to think in terms of money. At www.momclub.com, when women were asked why they decided to be a SAHM, 66 percent said they didn't want to leave their children, and it was what they were put on earth to do. An overwhelming 85 percent of moms say the number one advantage to staying home is being there for their kids.[4]

Counting the Cost in Second Incomes

Suzie is a bare-minimum example. When you crunch your numbers, you may discover other factors. Take a close look at these variables, and check the ones that apply to your situation. Then go back to the Working Mom Worksheet. and crunch the numbers a second, third, or fourth time.

Tax Brackets—Dan Akst, a writer for www.moneycentral.com says, "The main culprit for the financial failure of a second income is a tax system that savagely penalized second incomes."[5] For example, a second income pushes the couple from the 31 percent federal tax bracket to the 36 percent bracket.

Then add 8 percent in state taxes and another 8 percent in Social Security and Medicare taxes. Your job may put you over the limit and place your family in a higher tax bracket.

Commutes—You may commute farther than Suzie. Figure on $.48/mile if you drive (to cover fuel, maintenance, and wear and tear). That's $1,385 a year if your commute is a fifteen-mile round-trip.

Daycare—You may have more than one child in childcare—either all-day preschool or after-school care. The costs for these can range from $4,000 to $25,000 per year.

Food at Work—Don't stop at counting lunch costs. Add in the trips to the snack bar, sodas, and coffee during the day.

Convenience Foods—Your family may eat more convenience foods—most working couples do. But don't forget to add the fact that working moms are more likely to give their kids lunch money rather than prepare homemade sandwiches. This can add $1,000 or more per year for a family with two children.

Professional Upkeep—You may feel the pressure to have manicured nails, expensive suits, or additional personal perks—either because the work environment pressures you to have these or because you work so hard and deserve them.

Professional Image—Working moms are more likely to go to the expense of an "appropriate" car to keep up work appearances. Sales or real estate professions that require visits to a client, for example, may require the right kind of car.

Guilt Gifts—According to Linda Kelley, author of *Two Incomes and Still Broke?*, "Working couples, induced by guilt, often buy unnecessary things for their kids because they get so little time with them. Also, busy couples often don't have time to comparison shop."[6]

Dry Cleaning—A professional wardrobe may require dry cleaning that wouldn't be necessary to a home-based wardrobe.

Assessment—The most important part of this worksheet is to be honest and accurately assess your net usable income. Now go back over this list and ask, "Is the number I wrote down truly accurate for each item?" We'll come back to those numbers in the next chapter, as we refine the analysis and help you see whether becoming a one-income family is viable for you.

do we need a plan or can we wing it?

yes no

Half the Income, All the Benefits

SEVEN STEPS to Come Home

"Do you love me?"

"What?" I asked incredulously. I looked at my son and wondered if he was quoting a line from *Fiddler on the Roof* or if he was just playing a game.

He repeated, "Do you love me?"

"Of course I love you!" Since we had just watched the Fiddler movie, I started singing, "Do I love you? For seventeen years, I washed your clothes, fixed your food, bought your shoes. For seventeen years, I wiped your nose, if that's not love then who knows? Do I love you?"

I stopped my song and looked at him sitting at my desk. It dawned on me that he might not be kidding.

He held one of my books in his hands. "Then why don't you write anything about me in your books?"

"Of course I write about you in my books, Philip!" The idea that I favored one child over another was foreign to me. I went to great pains to see they all had equal time. Philip was obviously having a "Marcia! Marcia! Marcia!" case of the "middle-child" syndrome.

"I'm supposed to give this book to my friend, Erica, and how can I give her a book where there's nothing written about me?" He *was* serious; it wasn't one of his typical jokes. "I mean, all that's in here is stories about your adventures, Bethany writing on walls, Daniel shopping for bargains, Jonathan being so sweet, and how Joshua is always getting into mischief!"

I knew that wasn't the case, but it didn't matter, because it's how my large-footed son felt in his seventeenth year of life. "Philip, I wrote about how you were a drool bucket as a baby, and how you played banana smush in the hallway when you were three. I wrote about the time you were five and Christopher told you Easter was all about bunnies and eggs and not about the Resurrection, and you told him he was going to hell, and I had to redirect your enthusiasm. I wrote about when you were getting your first paper route and how you threw the papers on top of the roofs until you got the hang of it. I even wrote about how, as a two-year-old, you took the contents of one of your dirty diapers and smeared them on the side of the wing commander's new car." I sighed from the effort. "I've written a lot about you."

"Well," he replied, "I wish you'd let me write the foreword to your next book because you let Daniel write the intro to *Money Doesn't Grow on Trees.*" He readjusted his size-fifteen shoes, stuck out his lower lip, and looked a lot like the drool bucket he used to be.

"You can write a chapter story in my book about living on one income." I roughed his hair and tweaked his cheek, something he loathes. "In the meantime, I will make sure that I *never* write about how you say 'Yes, Mama, I'll fold the laundry,' and instead, you proceed to play video games and eat all the food you can find in the pantry."

He looked at me warily.

"Yeah, I'll bet you'd never write that." He smiled knowingly. "But I'll give you permission to write those things if you'll give me the money to go buy an orange mocha Frappuccino!"

He got the Frap—and the next chapter's intro story.

I'm a pushover when it comes to my kids.

****

When I think back on how Philip used to toddle around the house, sucking his thumb and dragging a threadbare red blanket, I wonder where the time has gone. I blinked my eyes and the toddler became a pimply-faced adolescent with crooked teeth and glasses. I blinked my eyes again and now he's got contacts covering cornflower blue eyes and perfectly straightened teeth that broaden into a clear-skinned smile.

When my six-feet-four-inch son and I walk into a store or the mall, I see girls swoon in his path—much to his practiced ignorance. He hates being called handsome and having us point out how the chickies respond to him. Some boys his age change girlfriends more often than Joshua changes his underwear—not Philip. He's also smart, a self-starter, and driven—with a 4.0 in school and a shot at valedictorian.

The amazing thing about this conversation with Philip was that he made me realize he needs me as much at seventeen as he did at seven months. Instead of changing poopy diapers, I help change poopy attitudes that could lead him down a path of negativity. Instead of feeding him strained peas, I strain to help him see himself the way God sees him. Instead of lifting him to reach the water fountain, I'm raising him to reach his full potential as an amazing member of the human race.

I would have missed much of this had Bob and I not decided to take the steps needed for us to live on one income. I didn't miss it. I was here.

For Philip.
And Daniel.
And Bethany.
And Jonathan.
And Joshua.
And Bob.
And Buddy.

****

Do We Need a Plan or Can We Wing It?

Nancy from California decided to stay home when she and her husband, Ron, had kids. They had a specific plan. "For the five years before Nick was born, we lived on half of what I made and put the other half in a savings account. Then we didn't 'need' my income. When Nick was born, we withdrew the same amount from savings. So we had five years of no pressure. By the end of the five years Ron was making enough money to fully support our family."

Jennifer from North Dakota had a different story. "When we decided to live on one income, we just thought it was the right thing to do, and it would somehow work itself out. Well, it didn't. We now have $15,000 in consumer debt, my husband feels financial pressure all the time, and our marriage is suffering. I feel that it's all because I'm at home and not in the workforce."

The point is: having a plan helps. Having no plan hurts.

You can modify your plan to meet your family's unique needs. While you may not have five years' worth of savings in your account like Nancy and Ron, you might want to set a goal of having at least six months of living expenses in a savings account before quitting that extra job. Most experts recommend a three-month pad, but for a family in transition—moving from two salaries to one—it's probably better to have six months in savings to take the pressure off during the transition. The point is: develop your own blueprint and build on it according to plan.

7 SEVEN STEPS to Create a SAHM

Remember, "A wise man counts the cost before he builds a tower" (see Luke 14:28). That's timeless advice. So the place to start is to access current assets, income, debt, and spending habits. The next few pages contain worksheets to help determine these critical numbers.

Feel free to scan the worksheet charts into your computer (to print copies), or make photocopies of the following pages. (Keep in mind that while you have permission to make copies for personal use, the material is still subject to copyright laws.) These worksheets are meant to be evaluated and re-evaluated regularly. They will guide you through the following steps:

1. **Current Income**—determine current income.

2. **Expenses**—assess current expenses.

3. **Assets**—determine ACV (actual cash value) of assets.

4. **Liabilities**—assess liability or debt load.

5. **Projected Income**—determine the new one-income requirement.

6. **Goal Expenses**—determine the new expenses.

7. **Variable Factors**—determine and factor in long-term savings, variable savings factors, asset liquidation, and a possible homemade income.

STEP ONE: What Is Your Current Income?—The first step is to assess current income. Go to figure 3.1, the Income Analysis chart, and write your current monthly household income. This would include all current income, tips, other earnings, dividend earnings (not subject to long-term savings), and other taxable income.

On the Variable question, write whether this income varies from month to month. For example, variable income would include commissions, tips that are not consistent, or dividend income that is not regular income.

Income Analysis (Steps One and Seven)		
© Ellie Kay (Figure 3.1)		
Step One: **Current Monthly Income**	**Amount**	**Variable?** **(Yes or No)**
Income 1		
Income 2		
Dividend/Interest/Royalty Income		
Other Income		
Other Income		
Total Current Income	**(Use this total amount for Step Five)**	

2 STEP TWO: What Are Your Current Monthly Expenses?—Next, fill out the Current Expense column under each expenditure in figure 3.2, Cost and Analysis Expense Chart. The monthly expense name and recommended percentages are given in the chart. The Current Expense you provide in that column may not line up with the percentages, and that's all right for now. We'll get to that in a later step. The point of this step is to find out what you are currently spending. It is important to know where you are, so you can get to where you need to go.

Keep in mind that the current expenses will likely include the second-income variables found in the previous chapter's Working Mom Worksheet (figure 2.1). Consequently, there is the need to include the additional expenses you currently pay for childcare, higher transportation rates, meals eaten out, the cost of maintaining a professional wardrobe, etc. These variables will reduce your overall cost of living once you are living on one income—and those will be factored in at a later step when you return to this chart. For now write the full amount in the appropriate space.

Include debt or credit card payments in the appropriate category. For example, car loans would be included under transportation. A vacation charged on your credit card (that you're now paying off) will fall under recreation/vacation. Consumer goods such as department store charges for a fall wardrobe would be included under clothing. Use the extra blanks for expenses not listed.

3 STEP THREE: What Are Your Current Assets?—The next step is to determine your current assets (figure 3.3). This is a time of reckoning when you are establishing net worth. Once this chart is completed, you'll have an idea of what you might be able to sell to accommodate the goal of living on one income. In rare cases, families find they need to move to a less expensive home or sell a newer car to pay cash for an older vehicle. We'll discuss these topics later.

As you complete this chart, you will need to do your "due diligence," a business term that means you follow through on the appropriate research to get an accurate number. For example, you may have more equity in your home than you think you do. Call your mortgage company and see what numbers they have. Then go

Cost and Analysis Expense Chart
(Steps Two, Six, and Seven)
© Ellie Kay (Figure 3.2)

Expense Category	Step Two: Current Expense	Step Six: Projected Expense	Step Six: Difference (Current-Projected =Difference)	Step Six: Goal Expense
Charitable contributions (10 percent)				
Savings/ Investments (10 percent)				
Clothing/ Dry Cleaning (5 percent)				
Education/ Miscellaneous (5 percent)				
Food (10 percent)				
Housing/ Utilities (30 percent)				
Insurance (5 percent)				
Medical/Dental (4 percent)				
Recreation/ Vacation/ Gifts/Christmas (6 percent)				
Transportation/ Car loan/Gas (10 percent)				
Debts (5 percent)				
TOTALS				

to a Web site such as www.zillow.com to get a rough idea of the fair market value of your home. Do the same for car loans and go to www.edmunds.com or www.kbb.com to determine the private-party value of your vehicles. You might find the car you think is an asset has little or no actual cash value due to the amount owed ratio versus the private-party value. Or you might find that a car you thought was worth $12,000 would bring $14,500.

For other assets such as antiques, electronics, or childhood baseball cards, go to www.ebay.com, www.froogle.com, or www.mysimon.com to get fair market values.

The final part of this step is a time of self-reflection. Are you willing to part with this asset to meet your one-income goal? You may not be required to do so once all the numbers are crunched, but the gut-level question is: Would you be willing to part with this material asset to venture into a *half-price living* adventure?

Asset Chart (Steps Three and Seven) © Ellie Kay (Figure 3.3)			
Asset Name	Amount Owed (if applicable)	Equity or ACV (Actual Cash Value)	Can Sell or Liquidate? (Yes or No)
Home			
Other Real Estate			
Savings	N/A		
Checking	N/A		
Mutual Funds	N/A		
Money Market	N/A		
Stocks/Bonds	N/A		
Retirement Plan	N/A		
Other Funds			
Cars			
Furniture			
Jewelry			
Household Goods			
Boat/RV/Luxury Items			
Antiques/Other			
TOTALS			

4 **STEP FOUR: What Are Your Current Liabilities?**—Most people don't know exactly how much they owe. The list of liabilities you provide from figure 3.4 gives an accurate picture of your current financial position. This also helps determine what you need to pay off before living on one income. The ideal situation is to be free of consumer debt and only carry mortgage and/or transportation debt. This will free you to establish a debt repayment schedule for each creditor and to decide which debts to pay off first.

Now is a good time to order a free copy of your credit report and check it against your records. You may think you owe $350 to JC Penney's, but the credit report may indicate you owe $750. This can have an impact on your (and your spouse's) FICO score (Fair Isaac and Company Credit Score), which determines everything from what premium you pay on your insurance bill to the interest rate on your mortgage to whether that future employer will hire your spouse.

Due to new federal consumer protection laws, each person is allowed to receive a free copy of his credit report every year from each of the credit bureaus. Since there are three major credit reporting bureaus, this means you can get a free copy every four months. Write down the following agencies in your planner or Palm Pilot to remind you to order one of the three free credit report copies every four months. This tip can save you big bucks and/or a major migraine when it comes to identity theft or other credit-related headaches.

All of these can be ordered at different times from the following address:

www.annualcreditreport.com   (877-322-8228)
Annual Credit Report Request Service
P.O. Box 105283
Atlanta, GA 30348-5283

For further reference:

Equifax (800-685-1111): www.equifax.com
Experian (888-397-3742): www.experian.com
TransUnion (800-916-8800): www.transunion.com

Liability Chart (Steps Four and Seven)
© Ellie Kay (Figure 3.4)

Liability/Loan	Total Balance Due	Minimum Payment	Months Until Payoff
Home			
Car 1			
Car 2			
Furniture			
Student Loans			
Boat/RV/Luxury Items			
Outstanding Taxes/IRS			
Department Store (list separately)			
Credit Cards (list separately)			
TOTALS			

5 STEP FIVE: Determine Your Projected "One Income"—In this step, refer to figure 3.5, the Projected One Income chart. Fill in the projected one-income amounts, leaving out any second income and including only consistent income such as the spouse's income, at-home-business income, and other income. You will take the total from this step and use it as a basis to determine the goal expenses in step six (figure 3.2).

After you've crunched the numbers several times, you may come back to this chart to add variable savings income (explained in step seven). So keep this chart handy.

Projected One Income (Step Five)		
© Ellie Kay (Figure 3.5)		
Step Five: **Projected Adjusted** **Monthly Income**	**Amount**	**Variable?** **(Yes or No)**
Income 1		
Dividend Earnings		
Variable Savings Income		
Other Income		
Other Income		
Total **Adjusted Income**	(Use this total amount for Step Six)	

6 **STEP SIX: Determine Goal Expenses**—This step is found on figure 3.2, the last column, and involves setting a goal for projected expenses that allows for an adjustment to one-income living. Return to step five and get the Total Adjusted Income number from figure 3.5. Take this number and apply the percentages given by each expense category and fill in the Projected Expense on figure 3.2. For example, if the new projected income is $40,000, then according to the percentages, the Housing/Utilities/Taxes expense would be:

$$\$40,000 \text{ x } 30 \text{ percent} \div 12 \text{ months} = \$1,000$$

The projected expense would be to have no more than $1,000 per month for the Housing/Utility/Taxes category.

Next, subtract the Projected Expense number from the Current Expense number and write the amount in the Difference column. This number shows you where you are and where you are going.

One caution: as you fill out this chart and get numbers that may disturb you, don't do the "the sky is falling" routine; keep in mind that these numbers are negotiable. They are, as they would say in the movie *Pirates of the Caribbean,* "more like guidelines than actual rules."

Finally, using the Difference column as a guide, tweak the numbers to fit your situation, and establish a realistic Goal Expense for your family. Put this amount in the final column. That is your new operating expense number.

7 **STEP SEVEN: Determine Variable Savings Factors**—In this step you will compare projected income with goal expenses and see how they line up. If you have more income than projected outgo, you can skip this step and go have an orange mocha Frappuccino.

If the projected income doesn't jive with the goal expense numbers, this is the step where you create your own plan based on the information you've accumulated from these charts. There's no "one-size-fits-all" for the adventure of *Half-Price Living,* and there will be as many variables as there are families reading this book.

Tonya, from California says, "If you want to make the change, you can—but you can't afford to wear expensive clothes, eat out at pricey restaurants, and drive new cars. I wear clothes from discount stores. There were times we collected extra change from the bottom of my purse for Taco Bell. I did without my own car for years (putting many miles on my double stroller), but I was with my children. Now our kids are almost grown. I can say I'm thrilled I spent so much time with them. I wasn't a perfect mother, but I was there. We have lots of great memories."

Terese, who worked in aerospace for twelve years, says, "By moving to one income, I no longer have the expense for travel, clothes, daycare, [and] lunches out. . . . I learned how to be frugal; I paid attention to many more details in running my home such as using coupons, paying attention to prices, learning how to make a meal last, and not being wasteful in any area. This was an awakening for me!"

If you don't have enough income, here are several variable options that may help you reach your goal:

Accurate Expenses: Go back through the numbers, making sure you've adjusted down the expenses to accommodate a one-income lifestyle. For example, if mom is no longer working in an office, she won't have the dry cleaning, childcare, or new wardrobe expenses from before. Go over these numbers carefully, making sure they are appropriately downsized to accurately reflect the new lifestyle.

Adjustable Expenses: There's no hard rule that you have to stick to the recommended goal expense percentages. If you don't need 30 percent for household expenses because your mortgage payment is lower, adjust it accordingly and move funds to recreation or clothing, for example. Or, if your spouse has a company car and doesn't need the full percentage for transportation, cut that and put more funding into a deprived category.

Variable Savings Income: This was mentioned earlier and is found on the Projected One Income chart (figure 3.5). This is where a family can make up the difference by learning to save money in all categories. The rest of this book will show you practical, easy ways to cut costs on just about everything on your expense chart. For example, after you read the section on saving money in the grocery store, you could set a new budget of 7 percent on food rather than 10 percent. Or, if you make the recommended phone calls to save money on insurance, you may find you're only spending 4 percent rather than 5 percent.

Variable Assets: Go back to the Asset Chart (figure 3.3) and look at the final column where you marked a "yes" or "no" on your assets. Is there anything you would be willing to sell to build the savings account safety net you need? Two words of caution when it comes to asset liquidation to accommodate one-income living:

1. Always consider tax ramifications before selling any assets.
2. Never sacrifice long-term assets for short-term living expenses.

In other words, if part of your personal plan is to open a HELOC (Home Equity Line of Credit) to buy groceries on one income—you need to change that plan. Or if you think, *I can cash in my 401(k)*, think again! It would be better to move to another home with a lower monthly payment than to cannibalize equity for living expenses.

You might need to consider selling that vanity car and trading it (and its high payment) for a reliable, paid-for vehicle. This would reduce monthly expenses. Simplify your assets, and maximize your savings.

Save While on Two: Recall that Nancy and Ron saved 50 percent of her income while she was working and gave themselves permission to use this savings as part of their monthly income when they made the move for her to stay home with their son. This may take higher-than-average self-control, but by the time their savings ran out, Ron was making enough money to fully support the family.

Variable Liabilities: Another factor that can improve your monthly expenses is to revisit your Liability Chart (figure 3.4). It's better to pay off as much debt as you can before you live on one income. If you can create a debt repayment plan for some of your liabilities, factor those numbers into your goal expenses; it can make up the difference. Are there any debts you can remove as luxury items? For example, Rob and Cindy, from Atlanta, used to have "his and her" Harleys before they had kids and while they were living on two incomes. "We decided to sell them to eliminate the monthly payments and help us with our goal of getting Cindy home before the twins arrived."

Another example is from Steve and Elizabeth of Florida, who used to have a ski boat (and a hefty monthly payment).

That wasn't a problem while she was an engineer and they didn't have children. But they decided to sell the boat and go skiing with friends to make the one-income lifestyle change.

Variable Income Factor: Consider an at-home business as a means of securing the SAHM status. In chapter 10, there are a variety of ways for the SAHM to make money at home while living primarily on the husband's one income. You are likely to find one that appeals to your area of strength and interest.

Seven Questions for Successful One-Income Living

1. In ten years will this _____(job, career, car, house, feeling, emotion, paycheck, wardrobe, lifestyle, vacation, etc.) matter more than time spent with the kids?

2. Not just: Is this a need or a want? But: Can I get by without this (consumable) item?

3. What is really important to me, to my spouse, to my kids?

4. What will I remember most about my kids when I'm retired and they are grown?

5. What will my kids remember most about their childhood when they are grown and bearing my grandchildren?

6. Do I spend myself into a second income and is it worth it?

7. Have I prayed and meditated about whether I should live on one income and how we can make that work?

you're eating on happy plates! you are supposed to be happy!

chapter 4

KiD buDget

HALF THE WORK,
All the Fun

The following story is written by Philip (the middle child) Kay

"Mom, wait up!" we yelled as she sprinted to the next roller coaster.

I'm a cross-country runner who can jog ten miles and barely break a sweat—and I couldn't even keep up with her.

"Hurry up, kids!" my mom called breathlessly. "We have to hit every coaster before the park closes!"

Something you need to understand about my mom is that she will make sure the roller coasters we ride are the scariest, fastest, and highest. My dad, a fighter pilot who flies thousands of feet into the sky at the speed of sound, and I, an aspiring Airborne trooper, dread those tall ones she drags us on. Like the one that suddenly shoots you a hundred feet in the air before you can say "holy moley" and whoosh! Off you go. But, hey, we all loved that one.

And so continued another wild and crazy Kay family day, but I love 'em. As my dad always says, "There is never a dull moment in the Kay family." How can there be a normal moment in a family consisting of five loud and ambitious kids with two adventurous parents? Some of our family vacations consist of going camping on the beach or in the Grand Canyon. Or the time we traveled the U.S. moving from New York to New Mexico and calling it a vacation. We stopped to see museums, parks, zoos, and even the Hershey's chocolate factory, where we purchased many valuable products.

There was one Fourth of July when we camped all day on the beach just to see the fireworks shoot off over the ocean . . . cool! Our Kay family fun carries its own traditions too. During Christmas in New York, we walked up and down the neighborhood, staring at the Christmas lights and listening to the carolers. Our faces were so cold we were afraid our smiles would freeze.

Nope, there's never a dull moment in our home. Most of my friends talk about just hanging out at home. Usually they show up to an empty house because their parents both work until 6 p.m., and their siblings are in daycare until 7 p.m. It always brings a smile to my face to be able to walk into the house and see my mom there. Sometimes she does an impression of my Spanish grandma and pinches me on the cheek while she perfectly imitates my grandma's outrageously funny accent. At the end of every day, the whole family will sit down to dinner and a family meeting. We'll share our favorite part of the day and sometimes eat on "Happy Plates" when someone has had a really good day.

Dinner often ends with everybody rolling on the floor, laughing at Mama's stories or at Daniel's funny jokes, or listening to Joshua's latest excuse of "how-I-think-I-may-have-accidentally-broken-the-school-water-fountain-but-I-don't-remember-and-you-might-get-a-call-from-the-principal" stories.

I hope you enjoy this chapter about the family meeting and that you can keep up with my mom. She really does practice what she preaches. Whether it's trying to keep up with her on the roller coasters or keep up with the latest story *du jour*, one thing is for sure: there's never a dull moment.

To find success in living on one income, the family needs to find the right pace and cooperate. Just as if everyone crawled into the same roller coaster car, all are on this ride together. Saving money, earning extra income, curbing wants and desires—all of these are ways family members actively contribute to the team. Anna, a mom from Arkansas, says, "So many children in our society are used to having pretty much anything they want. But by learning as a family to live *under* one income, we all learn the value of stewardship and self-sacrifice, rather than the pursuit of indulgence."

I recommend a family conference on the subject of finances about once a month. Items on the agenda can include any topic that needs extra attention. Some suggested ideas are: kid budgets; delegated responsibilities; brand-name guidelines; and brainstorming ways to save, earn, and spend money.

The first step to successful family meetings is to *hard schedule* a sacrosanct time on the calendar to indicate that family communication and team building is a priority in the home. The next step is to set boundaries that will foster open dialogue and feelings of cooperation. Here are some ideas that may help:

Ground Rules

A Refreshing Walk—Not a Marathon

One of the reasons some families disagree over money matters is they feel they have to solve all their problems in one sitting. This makes as much sense as trying to run the L.A. marathon with a two-mile running base. Families meetings are not going to be marathon sessions. They should only last *one hour*—tops.

The main consideration for optimum results is to keep the discussion moving. This is a time to learn to dialogue, without strife, on difficult topics. This isn't a time to solve all the financial issues in one meeting—that will come over time. There are some people (mostly guys) who want to fix problems immediately, but that's not the purpose of a meeting. Communication and open dialogue are the most important elements in these sessions.

Family Fun

To make this time fun, let family members plan different aspects of the meeting. One family may want to order pizza and another build their own sundaes after the meeting. Some may eat on "Happy Plates" (big yellow smiley face ceramic plates, purchased at the 99-cent store). I still remember breaking up a fight between my youngest boys by shouting, "You can't fight now! You're eating on happy plates! *You are supposed to be happy!*" That made them smile.

Synch the Calendars

It's important to have these meetings scheduled into the week or month. Every family meeting will include setting aside time to synch calendars for the next meeting. It's best to do this early in the session, just in case someone discovers, halfway through the meeting, they have turned into a super *crankypants* and no longer want to cooperate. (Sometimes it happens, especially if you have teens.)

Set aside the time to meet and make it a firm commitment that cannot be bumped at the slightest whim. Initially, while the foundation is being set, a family might want to meet twice a month and then work up to weekly until the team situation improves. Then the team can go on a maintenance schedule of one meeting per month.

Seek Professional Help

It might be a good idea to meet with a qualified financial counselor to get on a budget, pay down debt, and handle familial financial conflict. To find a financial counselor in your area, go to www.crown.org (where you also can find financial classes for individuals and couples), the local office of Consumer Credit Counseling Services at www.nfcc.org (800-388-2227); or the Association for Financial Counseling and Planning Education (AFCPE) at 614-485-9650 or www.afcpe.org. These are nonprofit organizations designed to help consumers with financial issues.

Seek to Understand Before Being Understood

This is taken straight out of Stephen Covey's *The Seven Habits of Highly Effective People.* There's a reason Covey sold a gazillion copies of that book—the principles work. It's important for family members to agree that they will try to understand what another family member is saying *before* they try to get others to understand what they are saying. There are certain phrases that communicate this best such as: "I hear you saying that. . ." and then repeat what you think the other person said. It's also important to confirm their meaning in, "You heard me right" or "You heard me wrong, what I was trying to say was. . ."[1]

The Patience Principle

Before beginning, each family member should agree to be patient with each other—it's only for sixty minutes. It's a good idea to go around the table and say, "I will try to be kind and patient during this meeting," or pass around a piece of paper with that statement written at the top and ask each family member to sign it. This is a verbal and/or tangible reminder of the attitude the family is adopting for the meeting.

"Win-Win" or "Agree to Disagree" Solutions

This is another Covey-ism. Any conflict can be resolved in one of several ways:

Win/Lose: One wins/the other loses

No Deal: There is a no-deal resolution where neither side wins and/or they agree to disagree.

Win/Win: Both sides win.

In the case of the family meeting, the objective is to go with the win/win or no-deal solution. It's a good idea to decide ahead of time, as a family, that there will be a positive resolution in the meeting—even if that resolution is simply to agree to disagree and revisit the issue at another time.

No Condescension Allowed

When someone makes a lame comment (I hate it when I do that) or reveals ignorance on a topic, it's important to correct without talking down to the other person—everyone is on the same team.

Ixne Ottenre

That's pig latin for "nix rotten." This exercise is much like a brainstorming session, where there's a free exchange of all kinds of ideas. Therefore, there aren't any rotten ideas, although there may be some unique approaches to age-old problems. In fact, some families may want to throw out outrageously funny (even bizarre) ideas just to lighten the discussion, spark creativity, and have fun.

Goal: Interdependence

It's been said that "he who controls the finances controls the home." The women I've known who imperiously control all the finances and haughtily give their husbands an allowance are generally not royally happy gals. I think many of these grande dames have taken the role by forfeiture—but boy, when they take it, they do run with it. Conversely, after I wrote *A Woman's Guide to Family Finance* I heard from hundreds of women who never saw the value of learning about finances or couldn't find an approach that explained it in a way they could understand. Some of these women were widowed or divorced, and they wished they had gained a working knowledge of money before they needed it in such a poignant way.

Remember the goal is *interdependence* where both spouses have a working understanding of their finances, and the rest of the family plays roles as well. This could work in a variety of ways: In some families one spouse pays the bills and the other balances the checkbook, while the kids help file records. In other families the financially skilled partner handles the money (male or female, it doesn't matter) but briefs their spouse on their status and seeks input in significant financial decisions.

Honesty

It's important to be honest during these family meetings. If there's a new suit in the closet that the credit card bill will reflect next month, let the other spouse know. If one family member doesn't understand a term or concept, honestly admit it and learn something new. It's important to share feelings that come out in association with money and express them in a nonthreatening, nonjudgmental way. Start to share healthy phrases such as "I'm frustrated by this budget, and I feel I can't spend money the way I want to"; or "I'm afraid we won't be able to pay the bills or send the kids to college, and I want to save all we can to feel safe."

Positive Reinforcement

The overwhelming majority of people like to be affirmed and have their good habits reinforced. Look for ways to express gratitude and value family members. Phrases that work at a family meeting are, "That's a great idea"; "That's an interesting thought"; and "You are clever to think of that."

Positive reinforcement works outside the family meeting as well. No affirmation is too small. If Brandon took out the trash, praise his work ethic. If Chloe pointed out that one brand of coffee filters was a better buy than the other, praise her ability to comparison shop. If Buddy* ate the store-brand dog treats without complaining, praise his sense of contentment.

One at a Time, Please

The family meeting may take awhile to get going and build momentum. There might be some ups and downs, and it's important to give everyone some time to get into the concept. One way to accomplish this goal is to cover one topic per meeting—not three or four.

Another "one at a time" factor is to set a ground rule that only one person speaks at a time. In the Air Force, they sometimes make the speaker put his hand in a bucket of ice water while speaking— it gets him to be short and concise. But hypothermia doesn't lend

*Buddy would be the dog—not the toddler.

itself to family fun. A more practical "one at a time" idea is to pass a potato when speaking and only the person holding the tater can talk.

Sample Topics for the Family Meeting

Half-Price Living sometimes requires a greater level of understanding among family members about finances. While it's important that children are given the information they are able to handle, it's also unfair to burden a child with adult financial stress. It might be a better idea to shelve the more involved or emotionally charged topics for a "couple time" talk and stick with more relevant money topics when the children are present.

Kid Budgets

The more children understand about a budget and how to stay on one, the greater their ability to help in their one-income family today and function in the real world tomorrow. I've long been an advocate of fun budgets for kids. For example, when a family goes to the zoo, each child has a budget (funded by the parents) that includes enough for admission, lunch, and snacks. If she spends less than what she is given—she gets to keep it. There may, of course, be a born saver in the crowd, like our Jonathan, who insists he'll just wait outside the zoo until the family is through, so he can save *all* his budget. (Sorry, Jonathan, nice try—you're coming in with us so you won't get kidnapped by a loose lion.)

In the family meeting the idea of kid budgets can be introduced, and the family can decide which budget they want to try. Brainstorming some ideas for budgets can be great fun. Some other examples of kid budgets include clothing (for teens), school supplies (per semester), theme parks (we did this for Disneyland— their eyes watered when we gave them $100 outside the park and they had to fork over $55 to get in the gate), movies, a trip to the mall, birthday gifts, and Christmas shopping.

Delegated Responsibilities

This topic *du jour* can be a lot of fun for the family while teaching kids the value of a work ethic. Each family member may have strengths that can be utilized to the family's full advantage. For example, if there's a child who loves to cook, he could be the family chef one night a week as his additional duty. There may also be regular duties that are assigned—the family meeting is the time to do this.

It's always a good idea to brainstorm job titles and let children volunteer for their areas of interest. The goal is to help the family in their *half-price living* adventure. Here are some fun ideas to get the brainstorm session started:

Le Chef—Cooks a meal (or more) a week.

Surfer Dude—Researches the best buy on Web sites and saves the family money in the process.

Cheetah Chick—A personal shopper who researches and reports good values at the mall, thrift shops, garage sales, and consignment stores.

Mega Shopper—Learns how to shop at the grocery store and organizes coupons and sales.

The Apprentice—Enters the family budget into a Quicken file or other financial computer program.

The Party Animal—Comes up with entertainment options within budget and may help plan (and research savings for) the family vacation.

Mr./Ms. Organizer—Develops a chore/responsibility chart and is in charge of filling it out (with the help of family members) during the family meeting.

The Family Scribe—Keeps track of the topics/dates/resolutions of each family meeting. See *Half-Price Living* tip.

The Snuggle Bunny—This is usually reserved for the youngest family member who may still be an infant or toddler and cannot do much more than give hugs and kisses and snuggles—a critical element in family unity.

Brand Names

In the family meeting the idea of brand-name guidelines may be introduced. This is the philosophy of "we pay for the item; you pay for the brand." For example, if the eleven-year-old wants new tennis shoes, the response is, "Our budget will allow for us to pay $30 toward a new pair of tennis shoes. If you want the Vans brand that cost $65, you'll need to pay for the brand—in this case that will cost you $35."

Joy from Texas agrees with this philosophy and adds, "On one income, we have to be wise in our spending, and it keeps our kids from becoming spoiled by having the ability to buy anything they want."

So . . . let them buy the brand name. It usually only takes one or two times before a child decides that saving six months of allowance for a brand name isn't worth it. Or, they may decide it *is* worth it, but at least they know how much longer it takes to earn the money to pay for the brand.

Brainstorming Session: Ways to Save Money

Brainstorming is a method of problem solving in which all members of the group spontaneously contribute ideas. This sparks creativity in a safe environment. There are no bad answers although there may be some funny or bizarre responses. The point is to get creative ideas flowing and let everyone contribute.

The brainstorming question of the day is: what are some practical, easy ways you can think of to save money? One child might want to take over the coupons and organize them to save money. Another might want to check the tire pressure on the cars (for better gas mileage). Still another may want to sell her younger brother into indentured servitude to raise money for a big-screen TV. It's amazing what your family can come up with when you make it fun and keep it upbeat.

Brainstorming Session: Ways to Earn Money

What are some ways family members can earn money? Kids can do yard work, be a dog walker, collect mail for neighbors who go out of town, babysit, wash cars, bake cookies, or have a lemonade stand. For ideas on kid jobs that suggest prices, materials needed, and safety factors, go to www.elliekay.com, click on Ellie the Author, and look under the page marked "Money Doesn't Grow on Trees."

But don't leave it there; go to chapter 10 and look for ideas on starting a home business to supplement a one-income lifestyle. The entire family could be in on the ground floor level of starting a homemade business.

Brainstorming Session: Ways to Spend Money

This may seem like an odd question—after all, one-income families want to *earn* or *save* money, not *spend* it, right? Wrong. It's important that family members have a measure of ownership in the way money is spent in the home—especially entertainment and vacation money. This is the time to brainstorm places to see and fun things to do—within the budget. Or, if it isn't affordable now, the family can determine how long it would take to save to make that dream vacation come true.

Family Meeting Notebook

Pick a date for your family meeting and a topic. Do this today. As a recap, here are some possible topics of discussion. Copy these, and put them in a Family Meeting Notebook. (The creative child can make this notebook.) Select a new family meeting date and new topic during each family meeting to keep the momentum going.

—Kid Budgets
—Delegated Responsibilities
—Guidelines for Brand Names
—Brainstorming Session: Ways to Save Money
—Brainstorming Session: Ways to Earn Money
—Brainstorming Session: Ways to Spend Money
—New Topic: _____
—New Topic: _____
—New Topic: _____

"you have to learn as Americans say to, 'chop on a chewstring'."

Chopping on a Chewstring

HOW TO CUT
Your Food Bill in Half

Forty years ago, my mom was a new military bride, who married my dad, a Navy third-class petty officer, while he was stationed in her home country of Spain. Mom is an amazing example of the foreign military spouse, but she's also a role model for all moms in her ability to be spunky, tell a funny story, and stand up for what she believes. Most military brides who immigrate to the United States face a double whammy: they must learn the military lifestyle *plus* a new culture, complete with different customs and often a new language.

But my mom who "loves to tell stories and make people laugh" coped by learning to look at the world through plastic glasses with a fake mustache and a funny nose—a gift she passed along to me. Besides teaching me how to look at the funny side of life, my mom also taught me a few things about shopping.

I remember when I was eight years old, she decided it was time for me to learn how to shop for bargains in the grocery store. I can still see her in her pink polka-dot seersucker dress and neatly kept short black hair. "*Leestin*, Ellie, I have to tell you *somethin'*," she said once we got to the store. "There is a secret to *chopping* at the store!" We walked to the produce section and she leaned in close, looking me in the eye. "*Chew* have to be a good *chopper*! Your father and I, when we first get married, we no have much money. We have to be smart and no buy no bananas that is too ripe or eggplant that is too mooshey. You need to *chop* wisely. You have to learn, as Americans say, to *'chop on a chewstring.'*"

To this day, I consider myself a smart chopper—I only buy green bananas, and I solved the eggplant dilemma by never buying it at all. This is a talent my mom passed on to me and that I'm passing along to my children.

One of the secrets of cutting a food bill in half is to layer the savings. If there is a foundational layer of savings, then another and another can be added to the previous layers until the item is almost free. While this isn't possible for all the household goods on a grocery list, up to 70 percent of the items in the store can be purchased at the right time for the right price by layering the savings.

When my son Jonathan was eleven, he became a great example of how kids can learn this technique and how savvy they can be. I took him to the store, and he wanted to do his own shopping. As we made our way toward the grocery store checkout, he looked up at me. "Can I go through a different line with my stuff by myself?"

I looked at our freckle-faced boy, his eyes lit with excitement. He was buying groceries for his sister and her new husband as the newlyweds set up the pantry in their first home.

"Sure, son. I'll be here when you're done."

After a few minutes, I heard a commotion in Jonathan's lane— the store manager, the checker, and a sacker were excited. When Jonathan finished, he was holding three grocery bags, and I asked him, "Honey, what happened over there?"

He smiled broadly. "Well, my total before coupons was $28.60, but afterwards it was only $1.80! They had a hard time believing I could save that much!" His grandma would have been proud of the way he could *chop on a chewstring.*

****

7 ELLIE'S Seven-Layer Recipe for Grocery Savings

If an eleven-year-old can learn to save money in the grocery store, so can you. Our family saved over $8,000 last year on food, toiletries, and cleansers. That is the equivalent of $13,500 earned on the economy (when deductions for social security and taxes are factored in).

There are seven savings layers that can be combined to save money on food, toiletries, cleansers, and other household products. The more of these factors that are combined, the more likely it is to get items for pennies or even free.

1 **LAYER ONE: Store Cards**—These are sometimes referred to as "clipless coupons." Sign up for the card at the customer service desk or online at their Web site, and scan it at the checkout to receive all the store's special values for the week.

2 **LAYER TWO: Sale Ads**—This is something most people saw their moms doing when they were growing up—I know I saw my *mamacita* poring over the ads with the intensity of a craftsman cutting a diamond. The store's weekly sale ads either come in the mail or are part of midweek newspaper inserts. Match sale ads with other savings layers for more savings. For weekly sales in any local community, go to the store's Web site.

3 **LAYER THREE: Manufacturer's Coupons**—These are traditional coupons issued and reimbursed by the manufacturer. Look at the fine print of the coupon to see the manufacturer's name and mailing address. Here are a few places to find these coupons:

> **FSIs**—(free-standing inserts) Most of these are in the Sunday paper. A family may want to consider purchasing multiple copies of this newspaper to get more FSIs. I buy four copies of the Sunday paper each week.
>
> **Blinkers**—These are the blinking dispensers in the grocery store aisle that disperse coupons for your convenience. Most

blinker coupons cannot be doubled at a double-coupon store. Gathering these coupons is a child-friendly job.

Products—Some products have coupons on the package that you can tear off and use immediately. Others require a purchase of the item to find the coupons inside the box or to cut them from the packaging.

Electronic—These coupons are issued at the checkout after the groceries have been purchased. They are usually competitor coupons automatically issued as a result of the consumer's choices. For example, last week I bought Quaker Toaster Treats (for $.60 a box with three different savings factors), and I received an electronic coupon for $.50 off Pop Tarts. I also bought Pedigree dog food and received a coupon for a free, eight-pound bag of Iams dog food.

4 **LAYER FOUR: Double Coupons**—Some stores offer double (or triple) coupons. This is where the coupon is worth twice the face value—so a $.50 coupon is now worth $1. The manufacturer reimburses the face value of the coupon and the store's marketing department reimburses the double portion. (You get double the value, but at least you know the background of the coupon offer.)

There are limitations issued by the store, such as they will "only double up to $1" or "double coupons limited to three like items." So check the customer service desk for details. Go to the links page at www.elliekay.com to find a link listing stores that double coupons in each state.

Some stores offer these every day, while others only offer double coupons on special days; check with the store to get the particulars, and time your purchases accordingly.

5 **LAYER FIVE: Store Coupons**—A true store coupon is issued by the store and reimbursed by the store's marketing department. It will either have the store's mailing address or no address on it, only the store name. A true store coupon can be combined with a

manufacturer's coupon on the same item. For example, at Walgreens Drug Store, there was a store coupon for "Secret Deodorant for $.99" and I had a "$1 off any Secret." When I combined these savings factors, the deodorant was free. Read the fine print before combining coupons.

6 **LAYER SIX: Unadvertised Sales and Clearances**—As much as 50 percent of the weeks' sales are not advertised. Check the store aisles for sales and clearance tags. Also, most stores have a bargain bin in the back. An added bonus is that when your family begins to get these products free, you'll be able to share them with those in need.

7 **LAYER SEVEN: Price Comping**—Some stores, including Super Wal-Marts, will offer what is commonly called "Price Comping"; in other words they'll match the price featured in local competitors' ads. I do this to save time and money when I want to buy all my products in one place, and I don't want to drive to four different stores to get the "loss leaders." (A loss leader is a front-page advertised sale item that is sold at a loss to the store, but it pays off by getting the consumer into that store for the rest of her shopping.)

Check with all the local grocery stores to see which ones honor competitor ads. I once found a store that would price comp, *and* take manufacturer's coupons, *and* double coupons *and* take store coupons *and* feature their own sales. I got *lots* of things free at that store. And then we moved—again.

Super Savers or Super Spenders?

Now that you have my seven-layer recipe for grocery savings, it's time to determine how your family ranks when it comes to saving on food and household items. How do you know if you're doing a good job in the grocery store or if your performance is severely average? The next area, projected savings, is a topic that attracts everyone's attention. The Cost of Food at Home chart (figure 5.1) was taken from the Family Economics and Nutrition Review. Go to www.usda.gov/cnpp/using3.html to get a version updated monthly.

This chart provides information on the United States average per capita cost of food at home for four spending levels. To compute a family's food costs, complete the following steps:

First, add all the family's grocery receipts for the last three months. In the absence of receipts or canceled checks, expenditures can be estimated. Trips to the convenience store should be added as well.

Then divide the total by three to compute a family's monthly food costs. This is the average amount spent per month on groceries.

Next, calculate your family's average spending amounts based on the criteria given in the chart. Note the use of age and gender in calculating a family's amounts. Compare your family's monthly spending habits with the four spending levels on the Cost of Food at Home chart.

Notes for chart on next page:

1. Assumes food for all meals and snacks is purchased at the store and prepared at home. Estimates for the thrifty food plan were computed from quantities of foods published in *Family Economics Review* 2006 (1). Estimates for the other plans were computed from quantities of foods published in *Family Economics Review* 2006 (2). The costs of the food plans are estimated by updating prices paid by households surveyed in USDA's Nationwide Food Consumption Survey. USDA updates these survey prices using information from the Bureau of Labor Statistics, CPI Detailed Report.
2. All costs are rounded to nearest 10 cents.
3. The costs given are for individuals in four-person families. For individuals in other size families, the following adjustments are suggested: One-person—add 20 percent; two-person—add 10 percent; three-person—add 5 percent; five- or six-person—subtract 5 percent; seven- or more-person—subtract 10 percent.

USDA Food Plans: Cost of Food at Home at Four Levels, U.S. Average, 2006[1]

Family Economics Review 2006, USDA Cost of Foot at Home Chart, Jan. 2006 (Figure 5.1)

AGE-GENDER GROUPS	Weekly Costs[2]				Monthly Cost[2]			
	Thrifty Plan	Low-Cost Plan	Moderate-Cost Plan	Liberal Plan	Thrifty Plan	Low-Cost Plan	Moderate Cost Plan	Liberal Plan
Individuals[3]								
Child:								
1 year	18.20	23.00	26.80	32.50	78.90	99.40	116.00	140.70
2 years	18.20	22.60	27.10	32.50	78.70	97.90	117.30	140.80
3–5 years	20.10	24.80	30.70	37.10	87.10	107.60	133.00	160.60
6–8 years	25.40	33.60	41.50	48.50	110.00	145.70	179.90	210.10
9–11 years	29.70	37.80	48.50	56.40	128.60	163.80	210.00	244.40
Male:								
12–14 years	30.90	42.70	52.80	62.60	134.00	185.00	228.70	271.10
15–19 years	32.20	44.20	55.00	64.10	139.40	191.50	238.20	277.60
20–50 years	34.20	44.00	54.90	67.10	148.30	190.70	237.80	290.70
51 years and over	31.30	42.00	51.70	62.40	135.70	181.90	224.10	270.40
Female:								
12–19 years	30.80	37.10	44.80	54.30	133.60	160.60	194.20	235.30
29–50 years	30.90	38.40	47.00	60.60	134.10	166.60	203.50	262.50
51 years and over	30.50	37.30	46.50	56.00	132.20	161.70	201.50	242.80
FAMILIES:								
FAMILY OF 2:								
20–50 years	71.70	90.70	112.00	140.40	310.60	393.10	485.40	608.40
51 years and over	68.00	87.20	108.10	130.30	294.70	378.00	468.20	564.50
FAMILY OF 4:								
Couple, 20–50 years and children—	103.40	129.90	159.60	197.20	448.20	562.90	691.50	854.50
2 and 3–5 years	120.30	153.90	191.80	232.60	521.10	666.80	831.20	1,007.70
6–8 and 9–11 years								

Food Cost Savings Projection

With this information, current spending levels can be compared with national averages in the four categories listed. A projected savings plan may also be computed. Using the layering plan, a family should be able to lower its spending level to the low-cost or the thrifty plan. These additional savings can be included in the variable savings plan when computing the Cost and Analysis Expense Chart (figure 3.2) from chapter 3.

Stretching One-Income Eating Out Nights

Who wants to cook every night? Not I, says the mama. But it's not always affordable to go out to eat, is it? Here are some ways to take a $100-a-month entertainment budget and stretch it to two times the fun:

FSIs—Free-standing inserts are the coupon inserts from your Sunday paper. Mainline restaurants offer great coupon values in FSIs that can add up to 50 percent off the bill, or almost $400 per year!

Newspapers—Scan the local newspaper's living or entertainment section and look for weekly restaurant specials. It may require going out on a Tuesday instead of Wednesday. What only takes about twenty seconds to check can save you $20 (or more).

Internet—Find a favorite restaurant's Web site, and check out their values. Many sites offer printable coupons and weekly specials. Go to your favorite restaurant's site and see if they have online specials. On my Web site at www.elliekay.com I have links to coupon sources that find local coupon values based on your zip code, or go to www.restuarant.com to buy discounted certificates and/or receive coupons for restaurant values.

Two for One/One for Two!—If a fave place doesn't offer a "buy one/get one free" special, why not try sharing a meal? This savvy approach is especially smart at a restaurant that's notorious for serving larger portions. There may be a small surcharge for an extra plate, but both wallets and waistlines will thank you.

Entertainment Books—These coupon books cost from $25 to $35 and are usually a great value. Go to www.entertainment.com to find local offers. Not only do they feature restaurant coupons, but they offer great values on local and national services, including theater tickets, movies, and sporting events. But be forewarned: they're not cost effective if you leave them at home.

School Discount Cards—These fund-raisers for both public and private schools usually cost between $10 and $15 and have dozens of stores/services listed on a credit-card sized card. Be sure to pay attention to limitations and have fun while helping a good cause.

Simplify—Save almost half the bill by doing three simple things: order water instead of soda or specialty drinks (it's healthier anyway), skip the appetizer (they usually serve bread instead), and eat dessert at home (the highest markup in a restaurant is on dessert). This tip will help reduce a $50 bill to only $25 for two people.

Bargaining 101

While we're on the topic of saving money while shopping, let's take a look at how to bargain while shopping for other items, such as jewelry, electronics, clothing, furniture, or just about anything. If you save money by paying less on consumer items, you could "earn" anywhere from $100 to $10,000 a year. It's a matter of learning how to negotiate on everything from shoes to salaries. Here are a few successful strategies:

Compare—Furniture, phone plans, electronics, jewelry, and appliances are all negotiable. Find your desired item on a search robot such as www.froogle.com, www.mysimon.com, www.nextag.com, and www.ebay.com, or in sale circulars from the Sunday paper. Then print out the price, take it into your store, and ask them to match it. Remember, some stores, such as Wal-Mart, automatically match competitors' ads (on more than just food items).

Compensate—If the salesperson can't match the price, ask for other freebies such as complimentary delivery, free accessories, or extended warranty.

Continue—If the salesman grants extra perks, don't stop there. After you've secured these, ask for the manager and ask her to match the competitor's price.

Counter—It never hurts to counter a price. If you ask for 20 percent off and they offer 10 percent, then counter with 15 percent. When it comes to salary negotiations, you shouldn't accept the first offer. Most salaried professionals ask for 10 percent to 12 percent more than what they're offered, and often settle for 7 percent to 8 percent more.

Consideration—Don't limit the odds of success by asking for too much. The store has to make a profit. Small appliances are usually marked up 30 percent, while larger ones such as washing machines are marginalized by only 15 percent. However, most large furniture items and jewelry are increased by a whopping 100 percent.

Communication—Learn to say: "Is this your best price?" "Was this recently on sale and can I have the sale price?" "Do you think you could ask your manager? I'll be happy to wait"; "Hmmm, this item is a little damaged (makeup on the collar, an already opened box, a ding or scratch); could it be marked down?" Once you've asked for a discount, don't speak. It may become a bit awkward, but a key rule of negotiation is: "He who speaks first, loses." And last but not least, when bargaining 101 is over, be sure to add "Thank you, I'll be back!"

stretch your clothing budget without having your children look like they've been outfitted by garage-sale rejects

A CLOTHESHORSE'S GUIDE
to Dressing Ponies

When I was a girl, I thought I'd grow up, marry my prince charming who would gallop into my life on a white steed, and we'd have the perfect family: two children—one boy and one girl. Instead, I was swept off my feet by a strapping fighter pilot. My fantasy of marriage and family was far from my reality.

I remember when Bob and I had our last baby and our oldest son was only seven. I was a former clotheshorse with an eye for a pretty bargain, and nothing in my closet would fit me but my pregnant clothes! I went through some pretty significant postpartum depression that left me wondering where God had gone. Things came to a chaotic climax one day while I was homeschooling the oldest three, nursing the baby, and keeping the toddler out of the toilet bowl. It was exhausting enough just trying to keep up with diaper changes for two babies without adding reading, writing, and arithmetic to the equation.

That afternoon, I laid the babies down for their naps, put the older children to work on school assignments, and barricaded myself in my bedroom for a good cry.

As I threw myself onto our quilt-covered bed, I sobbed, "God!

Why did you give me five children?" I pounded my pillow with my fist. "I didn't ask for that many. I thought two would be enough. Why did you give me *five*?"

My crying jag was rudely interrupted by a steady knocking on the door, accompanied by a chorus of "Mama! Hell-wo? Mama? Can we go to da paark, Mama? I want sum juuuice! Mama?"

I tried to ignore them, but that only lasted a couple of minutes. When I got up to open the door, I saw five sets of assorted-sized fingers—even the baby's—poking under the door. Our oldest had gotten the babies out of their beds in an attempt to garner sympathy for their cause.

As I looked at those chubby fingers writhing about like a bunch of silly worms, a still, small voice broke through my exhausted physical state with a radical thought, *Your blessings are not a burden. Let Me help you carry them.*

A single stream of light called "Hope" broke into my world, and I knew I already had everything I needed to love, train, and equip these special gifts God had given me. I just needed to lean a little more on Him and a lot less on me. That night, an angel named Brenda Taylor who had called to encourage me earlier in the day unexpectedly brought us dinner. Knowing I was dealing with postpartum depression, she arranged for someone else to bring a meal the next night. And the next. And the next.

Bob and I slowly worked to get our young family into a routine and eventually hope was restored. Sure, taking care of five small children was still exhausting and even maddening at times, but it got easier—in time.

****

According to the U.S. Census Bureau, in 1980 there were over 4 million families with three children. Twenty years later, there are over 7 million families with three *or more* children in the household. The trend for larger families is expected to continue for the generation of tomorrow's parents who will transition into adulthood during the early part of the twenty-first century. These college students are called "Generation 2001." According to a survey generated by Louis Harris and Associates for Northwestern Mutual Life Insurance Company, an incredible 91 percent of these hope to have *three or more* children.[1]

One of the greatest areas of financial concern in most families, especially larger families, is how to clothe all those children. One of my readers, Dawna, a mother of three young boys who admits to being a clotheshorse wrote: "Ellie, how do you make your clothing budget stretch without having your children look like they've been outfitted by garage-sale rejects? My stable of stallions is raring to go in style, but often faces the 'high-water' syndrome of hand-me-downs."

Top Tips to Outfitting All Your Ponies

Budget—This is basic, but if you don't already have a household budget with a clothing allowance, you're setting your family up for failure. The clothing allowance for most families is 5 to 8 percent of your total budget. Determine what this amount is and purpose to stay within it. This will cut debt and in the long run help to de-stress your financial situation.

Investment Purchases—For parents of more than one child, buying clothing should be a carefully considered investment. For example, cheaper is not necessarily better for three, four, or more children. If you spend $15 on jeans for Brandon (because they are superior quality) rather than $12 for a cheaper brand, they're going to last for Brandon's younger brother too. In the long run, higher-quality clothing can be passed down the line and will save you from having to spend an additional $12 on another pair of cheap jeans for the next sibling. Consider the quality, durability, and wear of the clothing you buy; and consider it an investment.

Unisex Clothing—If your children are different sexes, it's impossible to pass along clothing, right? Wrong. When you buy jeans for older children, try to get ones that are not gender specific. Do the same for coats, plain shirts, T-shirts, belts, even tennis shoes. There should be a few girlie clothes for your girls and manly clothes for your guys—but keep an eye out for as many items that can be intermatched as possible.

New-to-You Wardrobe—A creative approach to clothing your child is to trade out all the clothing you can't pass to your other children with another family. Look for people in your community or church who have quality clothing and a child who is a year or two older than the child you need to outfit. Then, see if they have a different child you can outfit from your child's outgrown clothing. Swap your quality clothing for theirs, and your child will have a new wardrobe. It's still important to get a few brand-new things for each child, so they will feel special and won't have to wear hand-me-downs all the time. But swapped clothing can be especially great for two categories of clothing: play clothes (which are going to be soiled and stained frequently) and church clothes (which are usually in better shape because they're not worn as often).

Don't Whine—Consign!—For an easy credit at your local consignment store, gather all your children's outgrown clothes and take them in. Be sure the pieces are clean, buttons are sewn on tightly (and all there), and that they are pressed if necessary—this extra care and effort will garner you a better credit. Then use that credit to purchase your child's clothing for the current season.

eBay Bounty

In 2004 more than 100,000 people made their living full time on eBay. You might be pleasantly surprised at the value a potential bidder places on what you may call a "castoff" (and they may call a "collectible"). Here are tips to keep in mind for buyer or sellers:

Tips for eBay Buyers

History—Check the seller's history before you buy. If others are unhappy with him, then pass.

Final Costs—If postage, handling, and insurance costs aren't listed, then ask.

Research—Compare prices by finding the same product at www.froogle.com before you bid.

Experience—Buy several items to gain experience before you start selling, so you can have high ratings as a buyer and seller.

Tips for eBay Sellers

Online Fees—Figure *all* fees into your asking price. There's a *listing fee*, a *final value fee*, and a *payment fee* when you accept an online payment.

Turbo Lister—Use this free eBay software to enhance product listing, layout, titles, images, and fees.

Photo—Invest in (or borrow) a good digital camera. Multiple images are often required to adequately show the item. Be clear on whether more than the first photo is free—you may have to pay a fee for additional photos.

Pricing and Duration—Decide how long your listing will run, the number of items in your product grouping, and the starting price. Never start the listing price of an item with hopes of getting more.

Disclose Flaws—Be sure to list thorough descriptions including dimensions. The more detailed you are, the more likely you'll have a satisfied buyer.

Disclose Fees—List postage, handling, and insurance fees.

Accepting Payments—You may accept credit cards through one of the online credit card services by registering at eBay.

Feedback—Cultivate a high seller rating through customer service and adequate descriptions. Always rate the buyer after the transaction is final.

Customer Service—Deliver products on time, and follow up after the sale. Determine ahead of time what your policy will be if the product is damaged in shipping. Are you going to cover it, or say "sorry—you didn't buy insurance."

Shipping—Get free boxes and priority mail packing tape through usps.com delivered to your door. The catch is that you have to ship the product priority mail, which is good if it's over a pound and under five pounds. If the item is over five pounds it is better to go with UPS ground or Fed Ex ground. Or buy boxes or shipping envelopes in bulk at www.usbox.com.

how do you like your nest eggs?

chapter: 7

HOW TO Make Cake
When Your Savings Takes a Beating

As a young mom, I was carrying a load of clean laundry down the hall when I heard strange noises coming from the kitchen.

"Ball, pop!" (giggles)

"Ball, pop!" (giggles)

I sensed danger and felt a sinking in my stomach as I rounded the corner and looked into the kitchen. My then-two-year-old son, Daniel, stood in front of the open door of the refrigerator gleefully dropping eggs one by one on the newly mopped kitchen floor.

****

Many Americans feel as if their financial nest egg has taken the same kind of beating in recent years that Daniel gave those hen eggs. So how does a family recover when its finances have landed in a slimy puddle on the unforgiving tile floor of a volatile market—especially when it comes to a one-income family trying to build savings and retirement accounts? While there are no quick cures or easy answers, there are some steps a one-income family can take to build the savings nest egg and prepare for retirement in an uncertain economy.

How Do You Like Your Nest Eggs?

Retirement Plans

In the 1950s there was one type of retirement plan—the pension plan based on years of service, salary, and retirement age. The employer sent the employee a retirement check each month out of the company's coffers. But since the 1980s there have been many more options available to employees. With the development of the 401(k) plan, employers were able to cut benefit costs and save money while the employees had the freedom to keep retirement savings (at least part, if not all) if they changed jobs. Today, there are three kinds of retirement plans:

Defined-Benefit—the traditional pension plan. For more information, go to www.pueblo.gsa.gov and ask for "Your Guaranteed Pension" to answer questions about the security of private pension plans, benefits, and termination.

Defined-Contribution—the 401(k) and 403(b) plans, SIMPLE IRA (Savings Incentive Match Plan for Employees of Small Employers), SEP (Simplified Employee Pension Plan) and ESOP (Employee Stock Ownership Plan). Most of these involve contributions from employees' gross income and employers match these contributions within guidelines.

Cash-Balance Plans—These are newly created hybrids of the other two plans. The employee may have an account into which employers make contributions but they act primarily as pensions, with a pool of assets and a formula used to determine a retiree's eventual payout.

One thing to keep in mind about all these plans is they are not necessarily permanent or 100-percent guaranteed. Granted, employers cannot take away earned retirement benefits, but they can reduce them as they go along. Therefore, it is important to keep an eye on revisions to employee benefits packages. For example, in the past few years larger corporations, such as General Motors, have cut back on or suspended their 401(k) matching contributions.

Eggs Over Easy
The 401(k) Plan

Most financial advisors consider the 401(k) one of the easiest investment plans for the average individual or family. The employee should ask the company to assign an automatic withdrawal for these funds from the paycheck, and, if possible, families should contribute the maximum amount allowed. Go to the human resources manager for an updated copy of the employee 401(k) benefits package to know how to take advantage of the company's plan. For example, when the employer matches 50 percent of the contribution up to 5 percent of the employee's annual $50,000 compensation, this means an additional $2,500 on the $2,500 the employee contributes to the plan. This is the equivalent of a 50-percent return on the investment.

Furthermore, the amount put into a 401(k) and its interest is tax deferred until the funds are withdrawn. Postponing taxes on earnings allows the nest egg to grow faster through the power of compounding interest. If there is ever a change of jobs, the employee should be aware of any "vesting rules" for the plan. Employees may not have access to contributions until they have worked the required number of years (for example, twelve months, two years, or even five years—depending on the rule) and become vested to receive benefits. Other defined contribution plans, such as the SIMPLE IRA, vest immediately; some companies also vest their employees immediately.

Changing jobs too quickly could mean losing part or all pension plan benefits or the employer's matching contributions. When changing jobs, the individual should roll over the 401(k) and not draw on the funds. For more information on 401(k) plans, call 1-888-8PUEBLO and request the free guide number 640N. This guide not only explains the numerous variations of the plan but helps employees understand what happens when they change employers and what to do if the money is needed before retirement.

Hard Boiled
The Traditional Certificate of Deposit

CDs usually earn more interest than a savings account and are a low-risk financial vehicle for retirement savings. They are insured up to $100,000 by the FDIC for all deposits at one institution. The money is kept on deposit for a fixed period of time and usually, the longer the term, the higher the interest rate. There are penalties for early withdrawal. Sharon Durling, a money coach and author of *A Girl and Her Money* (W Publishing Group, 2003) told me: "Unless you plan to retire soon, such as in the next one-to-five years, buying CDs for a retirement account is always going to be a bad idea, whether the economy is strong or whether it is weaker. The only time you would want to do this is if you have savings you need to use in the next few months or few years; [then] CDs become a great place to park your money."

As a rule, a one-income family needs at least three months of living expenses in a short-term savings account. Six months is even better. As for retirement savings, to calculate what will be needed for retirement to fill the gap between Social Security and pension income, go to any of the following sites and click on "Retirement" for an online calculator: www.crown.org, www.kiplinger.com, www.money.cnn.com, or www.usnews.com.

The Two-Minute Timer Egg
Individual Retirement Accounts (IRAs)

An individual retirement arrangement, or *IRA*, is a personal savings plan that provides tax advantages when a person sets aside money for retirement. The individual may be able to deduct some or all of the contributions to an IRA. Amounts in the IRA, including earnings, generally are not taxed until they are distributed. IRAs cannot be owned jointly. However, any amounts remaining in the IRA upon death can be paid to the designated beneficiary or beneficiaries.

To contribute to a traditional IRA, the individual must be under age seventy-and-a-half at the end of the tax year; and the individual or the spouse (if filing a joint return) must have taxable compensation, such as wages, salaries, commissions, tips, bonuses, or net income from self-employment. In addition, taxable alimony and separate maintenance payments received by an individual are treated as compensation for IRA purposes. By investing two minutes a day, a family can set up and manage an effective IRA account that offers a choice of investment options within the IRA, including stocks, bonds, or mutual funds. The contribution (through 2007) can be up to $4,000 a year (or $5,000 if over fifty years old) into a traditional individual retirement account on a tax-deductible basis. However, if the modified AGI (Adjusted Gross Income) is above a certain amount, the contribution limit may be reduced. Check with a tax professional as these amounts are subject to change from year to year. It's important to remember that individuals don't have to fully fund the IRA to its limit; they can always contribute less.

With a *Roth IRA*, the money put in is already taxed, but there are no taxes on the earnings as long as the account is open at least five years. As with the 401(k) funds, these accounts are tax-deferred and subject to a 10 percent IRS penalty for premature withdrawals (before age fifty-nine-and-a-half), plus there is tax on the amount (15 percent to 25 percent) depending upon the tax bracket.

How to Prepare for Retirement When the Egg Timer Is Ticking

Make Cake. It's not too late to use those broken eggs to make a cake; it's only too late if you don't begin at all. So if you haven't been investing, start today.

Low Cholesterol Eggs. Consider the other chapters in this book, and see how thousands of families are cutting expenses across the board and funneling the savings into their nest eggs. For example, try saving money on health insurance by going to ehealthinsurance.com.

Twenty Percent Beater. Try to put as much money as possible into tax-sheltered retirement plans and personal savings. The goal is to save 15 to 20 percent of the family income.

Pay Me Now; Pay Me Later. Consider setting up a homemade business to supplement savings (see chapter 10).

Aim High. That's not only the Air Force slogan; it should also be an investment goal. Families should not invest in anything they are uncomfortable with, but they should review their portfolio every quarter and try to squeeze out better returns wherever possible.

Sitting on the Nest Part-Time. The penalties for early retirement in Social Security benefits (see below), traditional pension plans, and funded 401(k) plans may mean the employee will have to work part-time before she can retire full-time.

Nesting News. Make full use of the home by renting out a room or moving to a less expensive home (or area) and save the profits. Go to www.zillow.com or the resource center at www.coldwellbanker.com for a Home Price Comparison Index tool that figures the cost of the family home in different parts of the country.

Simplify Your Life. Sometimes less can mean more. It might be important to live a less expensive lifestyle now to enjoy retirement more later.

Spring-Cleaning in the Nest. Sell assets that are not producing much income or growth, such as undeveloped land, a boat that isn't used, or an RV; and invest in income-producing assets.

Social Security Savings. Before individuals opt to receive reduced benefits at age 62, they need to be careful. The reduction is increasing to as much as 30 percent, depending upon the retiree's birth year—and the reduction is permanent. To research these benefits (the age to qualify for full benefits and the reduction in benefits for receiving benefits earlier), go to www.ssa.gov.

How to Hire a Tax Preparer

Not all good tax preparers or accountants are CPAs, but it's critical to find a tax specialist who is competent. Here are tips to finding a good one:

Who? It's important to ask around. Ask for recommendations from chamber of commerce friends, professional associates, church members, or small business owners in the community. Or go to www.crown.org to find a local Crown Financial Ministries instructor who may give advice or a referral to a good accountant in the area.

What? What experience do they have with individual returns or with small biz tax law (if there's a home-based business involved). Is he or she a CPA? If so, is the license current? Do the non-CPAs maintain their own DBA and small business licenses?

Another "what" question to consider is: What is a fair price? It could cost anywhere from $150 to $500 for a family return (including a modest small business), which would include preparation, Schedule C, state taxes, and advice on all other tax issues.

When? Don't go with a seasonal preparer (who does it only during tax time); pick someone who is year-round. While some of these tax specialists do a good job, many others are only nominally trained and disappear after April 15. It's hard to find an adequate seasonal preparer with a proven track record without a referral.

Where? A good resource can be found with the Better Business Bureau online at www.bbb.org. Here, the family can research a potential accounting office. If there is a home-based business involved, go to the local SBA office (Small Business Association) to get advice on finding a local CPA or tax adviser.

How? A lot can be determined through a personal interview. If they won't talk on the phone, their answers are vague, they won't give references or report how many small business clients they have—then go to someone else. It's reasonable to expect a tax professional to help reduce tax liability; advise on how to time certain purchases; know how much to invest in a traditional IRA, Roth IRA or SEP IRA; restructure a small business; advise on contract labor employees and home office deductions; and make other changes that help with taxes. Expect them to answer specific questions. If they just plug numbers into a program and can't report why—then it's better to go with Turbo Tax, because that's about all the tax preparer seems to be doing anyway. Tax preparers are being paid to know why they put in that number and what it means.

the wednesday factor . . . can be the best day of the week to get best price on everything!

POP CORN

POP CORN

POP CORN

HALF-PRICE Shopping to Maximize Savings

Joshua and Jonathan had just finished earning a ribbon for marksmanship in their Young Marines group. They spent dozens of hours over a period of four months studying weapon safety and history and having their knowledge tested with written and oral tests. They also went to the range multiple times, shooting at targets to improve their skill. Jonathan graduated with a distinction of sharpshooter, and Joshua qualified to receive marksman.

I knew Joshua had been spending a little bit too much time in this area of interest, but I had no idea how focused he'd become until I happened upon his creative writing project called "Leprechaun Stories," an assignment from Mrs. Drumheiser, his patient (and saintly) fifth-grade teacher.

Truth be told, I would have *never* found the story if I hadn't accidentally faxed a copy of it to my agent. Unbeknownst to me, Joshua made a copy of the story and left it in the fax machine. When I faxed my agent another document, "Leprechaun Stories" was still in the machine. My agent suggested I get eleven-year-old Joshua some professional help.

Picture a take-home paper with "Leprechaun Stories" preprinted on the top of the page and a cutesy little green guy with a pot of gold in the corner. Here's Joshua's work (spelling included):

Once upon a time . . . on a Wednesday . . . there was a Leprechaun who stole a pot of gold from the King. "King Evil of the dark ages."

A long name, you say. Yes you are right. But I made that up.

So he sent the secret police out, but they were actually terrorists. So they had a twelve-gauge, a G36, an assault rifle, and one guy had two P99s.

So they found him and started shooting at him. So the Leprechaun pulled out two oozies and a long battle begun (about four hours long.)

Then, when they were out of ammo, they stood up and became a team. It's a long story how. But they became a team.

So with two oozies, an AK-47, a 12 gauge, an M-16 (with grenade attachments) and a G-36, they invaded the palace and killed the king.

And there was piece in the land.

The End. . . . by Joshua Kay

I never figured out why this tragedy happened on a Wednesday, when St. Patrick's Day was on Friday—but somehow it made sense to Joshua. Maybe it's because he always has extra math homework on Wednesdays, and it makes him a little crazy. But there was a Wednesday factor in there somewhere.

****

There's another Wednesday factor that can help one-income families—it can be the best day of the week to get the lowest price on everything from travel to TVs to a new Toyota. In fact, there's a best time to buy just about everything if you just know when to spend.

Air Tickets

Wednesdays! Peter Greenberg of www.fodor.com says this is the best day to buy airline tickets, thanks to the small, upstart airlines.[1] In the airline business, fare wars usually are begun by the weakest competitors while the bigger airlines tend to raise fares. Fridays mark the beginning of new fare wars.

When Airline A decides to raise fares, it happens late in the day on Friday. By Saturday Airline A's major competitors will probably match that increase (that's why you should never book your tickets over a weekend). But what if the major competitors don't match the higher fares? Then Airline A drops fares again by late Sunday or Monday.

On the other hand, let's say the fare war is going in the down direction. Airline B decides to lower fares late on Friday. By Saturday and Sunday the other major airlines may lower their fares to compete. On Monday they are seeing how the new fares do in the marketplace. By Tuesday if the fares are doing well (meaning lots of sales), then Airline C might jump into the fray with an even lower fare. Prices may go even lower by Wednesday—and that's the day to buy.

By Thursday the fare wars and sales are usually over, and it begins all over again on Friday. The best time of the day on Wednesday is 1 a.m. (set the alarm), an hour past Tuesday and an hour past midnight, when most airlines usually reload their computers with the newest fares.

Cars

Most people know late summer and early fall is the time when carmakers release new models and dealers want to get rid of last year's leftovers. But most people don't know a good time to buy is at the end of the month and often in the middle of the week—Wednesday. If you can buy on the last Wednesday of the month, you'll do even better.

At the end of the month a dealership is anxious to meet quotas set by the manufacturer. If they meet their quotas, everyone's happy; but if they exceed their quota the dealership might be even happier because they've positioned themselves to get rewarded by the manufacturer and receive more of the hotter, better-selling vehicles next month.

End-of-month sales also can be consumer friendly because there may be competition within the dealership for a prize or cash incentive among sales personnel. The salesperson may be willing to cut commissions to win the bonus.

Another Wednesday factor is that dealerships aren't crowded in the middle of the week, and customers can get more attention from the sales staff. Early mornings and midweek are the least crowded times.

Entertainment

Wednesdays tend to be the lightest entertainment day. Many theaters, recreation parks, theme parks, restaurants, and museums have specials on Wednesdays to bring people out on "hump day." Look in the local newspaper or check the theater's online site to see what values are being offered. There are often "buy one/get one free" dinner entrees or "kids eat free" nights on—you guessed it—Wednesdays.

Houses

While Wednesday is a good day to look at a house because real estate agents tend to show fewer homes midweek, the best season to buy a house is in the winter. Steve Hargreaves, of CNN Money says, "It's best to bundle up when looking for the best deal on a house, as reduced demand and lackluster appearance can lead to a better deal in the winter."[2] There is a reduced demand at this time of year as no one wants to pull the kids out of school and move into a home when there's twelve inches of snow on the ground.

Houses tend to have a lackluster appearance in the winter and don't show as well. They lose curb appeal in their dormant state. Higher home prices come in the spring, when most houses go on the market. So buy in the winter and sell in the spring.

Toys

While it's hard to beat the post-Thanksgiving and Christmas toy sales, there is another good time of the year to buy—August. Not only can great deals be garnered on summer toys like playground equipment and swimming pools, but other high-space items are cleared out in preparation for the upcoming seasonal toy stock. This can save you as much as 65 percent.

Video Games

The season's new games are usually released during the holiday season, and that's the time to find the best selection. But if price is a consideration, wait until January or February, after the hysteria has died down and the savings can be more significant.

Televisions and Electronics

This last category may amaze you. Yes, blowout sales on electronics typically happen around the holidays, but April is an even better time to find deals in this category. Most Japanese companies end their fiscal year in March. This means new models are coming out and it's time to get rid of last year's models. Discounts for 20 to 25 percent can be had during this time of year.

Twelve Steps to Savings:

On Nikki Willhite's www.allthingsfrugal.com, I found a guide to special sales, sorted by month. I've added some of my own material, and here's a list that combines Nikki's suggestions with mine.

January

bedding	computers	quilts
blankets	holiday clearances	small appliances
calendars for the	(wedding gifts or	towels
current year (half-price)	gifts for children)	winter clothes

February

bedding
chocolate
coats
dinnerware
floor coverings
furniture
housewares
Valentines Day candy
  (after the fourteenth)

March

air conditioners
china
corned beef
dryers
frozen foods
garden supplies
glassware
houses
luggage
spring clothing and shoe sales
storm window clearances
washers
winter outdoor recreation
  equipment

April

Easter clothes and accessories
eggs
electronics
kitchen stove
paint
wallpaper

May

home maintenance items
linens
radios
spring cleaning supplies
TVs
towels

June

bedding
floor coverings
furniture
refrigerators

July

craft supplies
dryers
fabric
ground beef
hot dogs
sodas
summer clothing (clearance)
used cars
washers

August

bathing suits
fresh vegetables
kids' clothing
new cars
patio and lawn furniture
pens, pencils, paper
  (back to school)
rugs
summer footwear
towels and linens

swing sets
toys

September

backpacks
bicycles
china
gardening supply clearances
glassware
housewares
lunch boxes
root vegetables

October

crystal
fabrics
fishing gear
houses
rugs
school clothing (clearance)
silver

November

autumn decorations
blankets
flour
ham
heating devices and appliances
houses
quilts
sugar
turkey
winter outerwear (coats,
    hats/gloves, boots)

December

After-Christmas markdowns
    (shop for birthday, teacher
    gifts, Valentines, wedding,
    etc.)
flour
houses
party ware
sugar
seasonal decorations
    and tablecloths

inheritance. income tax refund. overtime. insurance dividend refund. pay raise. unexpected income.

debt

PAID

PAID

PAID

PAYMENT DUE

TEN STEPS to Simplify
Home and Hearth Expenses

They were chasing me. Again.

I could hear the angry, guttural breathing and heavy footsteps as I ran through the thick underbrush, my lungs burning with the effort. Why, oh why, did I ever agree to go on this adventur tour? They were going to catch me any second, and I couldn't escape. I never thought I would die this way. The hairs on the back of my neck stood up as I felt their breath against my skin. Just then, a strong, hairy hand from the 800-pound beast grabbed my shoulder.

I jumped up in bed, screaming.

My childhood nightmare had come back. Three huge, hairy gorillas were chasing me all over *Gilligan's Island.* They caught me every time. (There are consequences from watching too much "Nick @ Nite" while on a business trip.)

One of the things that hit me about that TV show was the fact that the millionaire was just as stranded on that island as the skipper. His money didn't change anything. The millionaire faced the same villains and challenges as everyone else on the island. He was forced to live as simply as the rest of the stranded crew. He just had nicer clothes, and Mrs. Howell had her jewels. But they still drank their coconut martinis from coconut-shell cups.

When it comes to our finances all of us are chased by the same 800-pound gorilla—whether we are millionaires or "thousandaires" (as my kids call us). The 800-pound gorilla in *half-price living* is the family home. If we aren't prepared to make the biggest payment in the family budget, it can be as frightening as being pursued by angry gorillas. Can't you just see their ugly black nostrils flaring and yellow slimy teeth snarling? (Sorry if you're a gorilla lover, but I think they're scary.)

Yes, it can be frightening for half-price (lily) livers like I am. But it doesn't have to be a nightmare, because that animal can be tamed.

****

10 ☞ TEN STEPS to Take Before You Buy or Refi

For couples who want to maximize their ability to get a good mortgage rate and qualify for the dream house they have in mind, there are practical ways to get there from here. One of the top things a family can do comes from Brian Israel, vice president of Chicago-based Harris Trust and Savings Bank's residential mortgage division: "Pay your bills on time. There is no single element that can so dramatically impact the success of an application as your credit history. Another thing, of course, is savings. People should have a good disciplined savings pattern. . . . That's the kind of behavior that's going to make them successful homeowners."[1]

Here are some more do's and don'ts from the experts.

1 **STEP ONE: Make On-Time Debt Payments**—This may sound simplistic, but it is true. If a couple is saving toward a home or a refinance, it's more important to pay the credit card bill on time before they pay the light bill if they want to qualify for the better mortgage rate. Every thirty-, sixty-, or ninety-day delinquency on a loan or credit card is going to reduce the credit score on their report. This is a consideration the loan officer will take into account when approving the mortgage, the amount of the loan, and the rate.

To make sure credit card payments are paid on time, the consumer should set up an automatic payment online that will cover the minimum balance due. If the amount set to draft is for a minimum payment, any additional payments (to pay down the debt—thus helping the credit rating even more) can be made later in the month. But at least the basic credit payment will be flagged as "on time," and you'll eliminate late fees.

2 **STEP TWO: Don't Miss It . . . but If You Do**—If as a one-income family you run into an adjustment glitch, a gap in employment, a medical emergency, or some other unexpected financial issue and must completely miss a monthly loan payment—be strategic in prioritizing the missed payment. Here is the priority level of missed payments:

1. The credit card payment would be the first to miss.

2. The second payment missed would be on an installment loan.

3. The final payment would be for an existing mortgage.

According to Michael Larsen, a writer for Money Central, "That's because credit-scoring systems look at the performance of similar loans first when deciding what type of score to assign. It will give the most weight to the performance of another mortgage, for example, than the performance of something like an auto loan, which features fixed payments and a fixed rate the way many mortgages do."[2]

3 **STEP THREE: Pay Off Debt**—It's important for a one-income family to pay off as many smaller debts as you can so that when you apply for a mortgage, you'll have a better chance at getting a good rate. Even if you put down a smaller amount at closing and end up with a larger mortgage, you'll be better off than the high-interest rates of most consumer debt. If a couple is pursuing paying down debt, they are in common company. Larry Hamilton, executive officer of SouthTrust's mortgage lending division in Birmingham, Alabama, said consumers are "putting less equity in

their homes, borrowing more against their homes, and they're paying off consumer debt."[3]

4 **STEP FOUR: Make the Mortgage the Top Priority**—If a family has a new job and the means to secure multiple loans (such as a mortgage, new car, and new credit cards), they should secure the mortgage loan first. Whenever credit is scored, each application for credit becomes a liability to the rating. Numerous credit inquiries, such as these, can hurt overall credit score, especially if filed in the months prior to the mortgage loan review process.

5 **STEP FIVE: Save, Save, Save**—It is best to increase the size of the down payment by saving as much as possible ahead of securing the loan (see chapter 8, "How to Maximize Savings"). Couples should invest these savings in secure accounts that offer reasonable rates of return, automatic payroll deductions, or other financial incentives to save. Once consumer debt has been paid off, these savings can be put toward a home down payment.

Consider the following six sources of income that can be applied toward paying down debt:

1. inheritance

2. income tax refund

3. overtime

4. bonus

5. insurance dividend refund

6. pay raise

7. any other unexpected income

6 **STEP SIX: Avoid Big Purchases**—A loan secured for a large purchase (such as a $15,000 auto loan) may prevent a couple from qualifying for the mortgage amount they want or negatively impact their rate. Lenders do not look favorably on adding debt upon debt. Besides, the more money a one-income family is spending on loans, the less they will have to put toward a mortgage. The best car to drive is usually the paid-for car a family owns now—especially if it translates into a more affordable rate on the family home.

Most experts say you want your total debt obligation including mortgage to be no more than 36 percent of your gross monthly income. You don't want to load up on consumer debt if you're anticipating the purchase of a home, you're unsure what your mortgage payment is going to be, or you think you're near that 36-percent requirement. I think 36 percent may be a bit high, especially for a one-income family; the intermediate goal should be to see debt at no more than 30 percent of gross monthly income with 25 percent as the ultimate goal. This allows breathing room for home and hearth to account for taxes and insurance.

7 STEP SEVEN: Live Within Your Means—Both Now and Later —Obtaining a mortgage can be like gambling if the consumer doesn't know:

1. how credit ratings are scored;

2. how much of a loan one income will support;

3. how much the new mortgage payment would be compared to the existing one.

For example, if a one-income family shoots for a loan that would raise the payments from $500 in rent to $1,500 per month in a payment (principal, interest, and insurance), they are likely to experience payment shock. A lender will look at this differential, and the family could find themselves in one of two situations:

—they might not qualify for the loan, or

—they might have to cover too much loan with too little money.

One final note: Those seeking to live on one income who plan to purchase their home while they still have two incomes (before they downsize to one income) need to determine the amount of the mortgage they will accept based on one income, not two. On two incomes they will qualify for a larger loan and maybe better interest. They can take the better interest rate, but should settle for a lower mortgage amount and perhaps a less expensive home within that one-income price range. For example, if the Schmidt family qualifies for a $250,000 mortgage based on their dual income, but plans to live on one income in the next three years, the family should go with the $175,000 mortgage (at a lower interest rate) that Mr. Schmidt qualifies for based on his income alone.

8 STEP EIGHT: Pre-Qualified Versus Pre-Approved—By pre-*qualifying* for a loan, the consumer is given an estimate of how much of a loan they qualify for after they've submitted income, credit, and debt information. In this case the lender does not pull credit reports, check debt-to-income ratios, or perform other underwriting steps. Rather, by getting pre-*approved*, these latter steps are performed and you are closer to obtaining a loan and locking in a rate and term. The first is an estimate; the latter is closer to the final product. Consumers should not get pre-approved until serious about their time frame for purchasing a home. If they are certain they are going to buy within the next sixty days, getting pre-approved instead of just pre-qualified can be an advantage.

9 STEP NINE: Don't Forget Money Personalities—Each family has a unique money personality. Consumers may forget this when it comes to getting a mortgage loan. If a consumer takes out a thirty-year fixed-rate loan rather than a fifteen-year loan, and if this consumer invests the money saved on monthly payments, they might earn a higher return on their money in the long run. To get an idea of the difference between a fifteen-year versus a thirty-year mortgage, go to www.bankrate.com, the primary place for rates and calculations.

However, few money personalities have this kind of discipline. If the couple's money personality is such that they tend to spend extra money rather than invest it, they would be better off getting the shorter term, forcing themselves to invest their money toward paying the house off in a shorter time.

10 **STEP TEN: Hidden Burdens**—Home buyers shouldn't forget the extras involved in ownership. Set aside funds to cover short-term and long-term repairs and maintenance; when something breaks, the homeowner will pay to have it repaired or replaced. Keep this in mind if considering an older home or a repossessed property. Home ownership also brings the responsibility of greater financial accountability. For example, missing a rent payment carries a smaller penalty than defaulting on a loan. Additionally, some first-time homeowners find themselves in a higher-interest bracket when it comes to credit card accounts.

*bonus **BONUS STEP: Variable Savings Factor—Half the Headache, Not Half the Home**—The American Dream seems to require moving up to arrive in life. But if the house keeps you running and stressed more than an 800-pound gorilla, how is that high living? On the other hand, who wants to move down to a lower house payment that requires a smaller, older, or less adequate home? That's why I came up with a third option: move over.

Another family I worked with in the reality TV series was serious about wanting mom to stay home with their children. But between child support payments (his) and the expenses of another child who lived with them (hers from a previous marriage), they had to make a move. They were living in a dream house in a brand-new neighborhood with a gorgeous view of a forest. It was *beautifulicious.*

They moved to an equal-sized house (which they needed) in a slightly older, but quaint neighborhood. This lowered their mortgage payments enough for mom to stay home with the children. It wasn't easy; I could see how hard it was for this woman to leave her dream home, but it was for another dream: being home with her kids. In the long run they were in a better position to save for

*This tip helps positively change the "variable savings factor" in figure 3.5 and/or the "goal expense" in figure 3.2.

a down payment on their next mortgage when they had paid down debt and his small-business income continued to increase.

Sometimes contentment lies in how you view your situation and what you are willing to trade for those things that matter most in life.

5 ☞ FIVE SAVVY IDEAS to Improve the Value of Your Home and Hearth

1. Slapping on Paint

This is the number one home-improvement project homeowners will try themselves. There are two keys to a good paint job: choosing the paint and prepping the surface. Splurge on quality paint, as well as brushes and rollers. If you're not sure of the color you want, rent a sample (yes, most full-service hardware stores will let you do this).

Prep the surface by cleaning walls, sanding them, and patching holes. This accounts for the majority of the work and will make your house show better (improving its value).

2. Finish the Basement

A family can add as much as a third more space to a two-story house for a moderate cost (only a fraction of what it would cost to build a third onto a home) and recoup as much as 80 percent of the investment upon selling. The first step to success is determining the basement's condition—primarily waterproofing. If a sheet of plastic wrap is taped to the concrete floor overnight and there are moisture beads on it the next morning, a waterproofing company might need to be employed.

It's critical that the basement have a sump pump (in good working order), as well as a backup. It's also important to check with the homeowner insurance provider to see if they fully cover the contents and materials in a flooded basement.

The final key to a quality renovation in the basement is to make sure there is adequate heating and cooling that doesn't drain the other units. A heating and cooling contractor should be able to design these changes to make them work, but get an estimate before going forward with the project.

3. Lose the Kitchen Wall

Many older homes used to have a wall that separates the dining room and kitchen. By knocking down that wall, the space is opened and *voila!* A new look that can allow you to recover 70 to 80 percent of the cost of renovation. The rest of the kitchen may need to be updated with wood cabinets, non-laminate countertops (such as Corian or Wilsonart) and non-vinyl flooring. Additional extras popular with homebuyers would be island seating, industrial-look appliances and heavy-duty drawer hardware. Mitchel Gold, a designer whose work is featured in Pottery Barn and Crate and Barrel stores said he once bought two stainless steel Fridgidaire stoves for half of what it cost to buy a huge Viking oven and range.[4] The result was that he had two ovens, eight burners, and half the bill.

4. Try a Little Bathroom Remodel

Keep up with today's amenities by updating your bathroom with double sinks, brushed nickel fixtures, powerful multi-head showers, and toilets in their own alcoves. Rather than spending $30,000 on a complete overhaul, you could purchase a new toilet, sink, and fixtures for $6,000 to $7,000. Consider getting an acrylic mold shaped to the curve of your existing tub and slipped over the top. Install a new drain and everything is fitted together with a professional-looking finish. But be sure there is no water damage behind the existing walls before you go with this idea. It can save you several thousand dollars over the price of purchasing and making space for a new tub. One family I talked to had their porcelain tub refinished by a professional nearly eighteen years ago, and it hasn't stained once since.

5. Window Treatments

When we purchased our current home, one of the main features the real estate broker, the seller, and the neighbors kept talking about was the windows. They were double-paned Pella windows, which was as nice an accessory to a home as a Prada handbag is to a fashion maven.

According to Jean Sherman Chatsky, "Name-brand windows can be a huge selling point to potential home buyers. If you don't believe us, just flip though your newspaper's Sunday real estate section. We bet you'll find window-brand names like Andersen, Pella, and Marvin listed by the real estate agents, along with the houses' other salient features (pool, hardwood floors, Sub-Zero fridge). This investment will pay you back in spades."[5] *Remodeling* magazine predicts a 75-percent recoup upon selling.

TEN QUESTIONS to Ask
When Hiring a Contractor[6]

1. *How long have you been in business?* Go with an established contractor, and check it out with consumer protection officials to see if there are any outstanding complaints on file.

2. *Are you licensed and registered with the state?* Only thirty-six states require licensing by contractors. Check with your local building department or consumer protection agency to see what your state requirements are. Ask to see the license.

3. *How many projects like mine have you completed in the last year?* Ask for a list.

4. *Will my project require a permit?* Most projects require permits; a competent contractor will get all the necessary permits before starting work. Don't hire him if he asks you to get the permits.

5. *May I have a list of references?* Call at least three previous clients and ask to see their results. Ask the clients if there were unexpected costs, if the work was completed on time, if the workers showed up on time, and if they would recommend the contractor again.

6. *May I see other jobs in progress?* Buyer beware if you're not allowed to go see the site or if the contractor doesn't have any other work.

7. *Will you be using subcontractors on the project?* If yes, then ask to meet them. Ask the subcontractors if they were treated fairly and paid on time. Subcontractors could put a "mechanic's lien" on your property if the contractor doesn't pay them.

8. *What types of insurance do you carry?* They should have personal liability, workers' compensation, and property damage coverage. Ask for copies of insurance certification. Don't work with the contractor if he won't carry insurance.

9. *What kind of down payment do you require?* Try to limit your down payment. Some state laws limit the amount of money a contractor can request as down payment.

10. *What kind of payment schedule do you offer?* Try to get this in writing on the contract (always sign a contract), and try to make payments due during the project upon completion of a certain amount of work. Never make a final payment or sign an affidavit of final release until you are satisfied with the work and know the subcontractors and suppliers have been paid.

Here are some other resources:

National Association of Home Builders Remodelers Council: www. nahb.com. To order a free copy of "How to find a Professional Remodeler" send a SASE to:

NAHB Remodelors Council
Dept FT
1201 15th St, NW
Washington, DC 20005

National Association of Consumer Agency Administrators:
www.nacaanet.net
1010 Vermont Ave, NW
Suite 514
Washington, DC 20005
E-mail: nacaa@erols.com

Are You Paying Too Much for Mortgage Fees?

A new National Mortgage Complaint Center (a watchdog organization that helps consumers avoid overcharges) study that collected data from more than 10,000 recent borrowers determined that overcharges and dubious fees may mean many consumers are overpaying to get mortgages. Here are the most common mortgage overages and how to avoid them[7]:

Inflated Credit-Report and Courier Fees

Some lenders are charging up to $65 for pulling your credit report. That is unusually high since credit-reporting bureaus charge $6 to $18 per report. Using the same tactics, some lenders charge courier fees of as much as $100 for shipping your closing documents, while the majority of overnight express services only charge $22.

Answer: Tell your lender, up front, that you refuse to pay any more than the going rate for these services.

Document Prep and Administration Fees

The origination fee should include these services, so don't pay them.

Answer: Ask your lender to waive these fees.

Yield Spread Premiums

Lenders increase your interest rate slightly to include origination and other fees so you don't have to pay them out-of-pocket at closing, but some lenders and mortgage brokers are double-dipping —charging both the fees and the higher interest rate.

Answer: Ask your broker if a firm charges a yield spread premium. If so, you shouldn't pay any additional fees.

Padded Title Insurance Fees

When shopping for lenders, look for all the above, plus look out for those who tack on a lot of extra charges for services such as title search and document preparation. Theses can add hundreds of dollars to your closing costs, and they really should be included in the price of title insurance, which, depending on where you live, can be as high as $6,000.

with imagination and talent, a hobby can become a source of income.

HOW TO OWN a Home Business That Doesn't Own You

I've been around. From California to New York and back to California with about thirteen moves stuck in for good measure. I've lived and shopped all over the United States. Imagine getting in line behind me, aka the "Savings Queen," in the checkout line.

After the groceries have been scanned and the checker is beginning to deduct coupons, it appears—to the average shopper—that I'm almost finished. You see, when I'm on a "regular" shop (and not a "short" shop) it usually takes a good checker twenty minutes to deduct my coupons. It's worth the wait. A technique I regularly follow (as should you) is to warn people in line behind me.

One time I went to the grocery store and got in the line of my favorite checker—Heather. The last few products were on the grocery belt when an older woman with eight items walked up behind me. Courtesy demanded I warn her. "Excuse me, ma'am. I have a lot of coupons. You would probably get checked out faster if you went to the express line."

Still holding her vegetables above the grocery belt, the woman stared at me in disbelief. I didn't understand her annoyed facial expression. *I haven't been in this town long, but don't they talk to folks in line in this state? I was polite, wasn't I?*

Whatever the case, I was sure of one thing—I had offended her.

She snapped, "I use coupons too." As if to make her point, she adjusted the net on her gray hair bun with a firm shake, and waved a Geritol coupon under my nose.

With angry determination, she continued placing her produce on the belt.

I smiled my sweetest little-girl smile. Maybe she'd like me better if she thought of me as a granddaughter. "I'm sure you do, but I use a *lot* of coupons. This is kind of like a business to me, and it's going to take the checker a long time to deduct all of them." I held up my overstuffed coupon envelope to show her.

I was unprepared for her emotional response. She gave me a ferocious glare, shaking her zucchini at me like a Samurai warrior, and announced through clenched teeth, "I told you. I use coupons too! Now, why don't you just mind your own business and let me mind mine!"

I got the point. I wondered if it was against the law to wield a zucchini as a deadly weapon. As Heather scanned my last few items, the older woman seethed at the "audacity of young people these days." She arranged and rearranged her produce and vitamins on the conveyor belt.

Heather had not heard the verbal assault. "Ellie, can I have your coupons now?"

I walked around the corner to Heather and handed her the contents of my coupon envelope. The woman with an attitude looked somewhat surprised at the pile of coupons.

Heather looked down at the big pile and whispered confidentially to the lady, "Ellie really does use coupons! We call her the Coupon Queen! It's her part-time job!" She began ringing in one coupon after another—and another—and another—and another.

The lady's face showed frustration; she hadn't realized I had so many coupons. Then confusion set in. Should she pick up her veggies and change lanes? Or should she stay where she was? Resolution settled into her thin features as she seemed to reason, *I'll just stay put. How much longer can it be?*

Another five minutes and wonder crept into her face. She couldn't stand it. She broke the silence, "You say this is a business for you? Have I seen you on Oprah?"

She straightened her hair. "Are you one of those people who buys all kinds of groceries for next to nothing?" She was openly curious now.

After Heather finished, Mrs. Hairbun asked, "Well, how much did she save anyway?"

The checker proudly announced, "The bill was around $150 and she paid $50, so she saved over $100."

Her mouth shaped a small "o" in surprise.

As I turned to leave, she put a staying hand on my arm, "You're right, girl. *You use coupons!*"

****

When Bob and I got married and I decided to stay home with all the babies who just kept arriving one after another, I never dreamed my hobby of shopping, saving money, and couponing would eventually land me a fun career that has helped thousands of families around the globe. But that's what God does: He takes our problems, helps us solve them, and allows us to help others learn what we've learned.

Saving money is still a hobby, even though it is also a business for me these days. I'm writing books, being interviewed on the radio and TV, speaking to live events, and even working for corporations as a consultant and spokesperson. I tried cross-stitching as a hobby, but I can't sit still long enough. I used to play racquetball, but it's easier to just go on four-mile walks with the puppy. I used to collect ceramic cats, but now we have a dog. The only real hobby I've kept is couponing.

The best home business a SAHM can have is pursuing a hobby or a passion that is enjoyable. This chapter features several SAHMs who have discovered that their passion can make for pleasurable and profitable home-based businesses.

But you thought this book was about one-income living? Isn't a home business a second income? This book *is* about one-income living—but it's also about stay-at-home moms who want to supplement that one income. One of the advantages available to a stay-at-home mom, as we saw in earlier chapters, is that she has the freedom to develop and pursue other interests. Some of these interests may help other people in a meaningful way or make that mom feel like she's using her God-given gifts productively.

According to Ann Crittenden, author of *The Price of Motherhood: Why the Most Important Job in the World Is Still the Least Valued,* "Forty-five percent of all businesses owned by women are based at home."[1] Ann is a former economics reporter for the *New York Times.* She estimates she "gave up" her income, retirement savings, pension, and other benefits to the tune $700,000. But she goes on record as saying she didn't regret a minute she had with her son. She also followed her passion into a new freelance writing business that opened doors for her while she was staying home.

It's okay if some of these passions and interests end up making money for the family coffers. It's also all right if a mom finds success in her home-based business.

One of the best resources for stay-at-home moms is *Homemade Business* by Donna Partow, who stresses the need to do research in the areas that interest you. She suggests:

—Ask your librarian to help research your chosen field.

—Look up books, magazines, and newspaper articles.

—Talk to other people who have done what you'd like to do.

—Join an industry organization.

—Subscribe to industry publications.[2]

The first part of research is to determine passions and interests. Women should consider taking a personal-skills-and-interest inventory. One such free assessment, Personality I.D., is a new and validated interactive personality assessment tool that allows the respondent to view herself and others from a fresh perspective. Its purpose is to help the individual identify and understand her unique personality. By understanding personality and how it causes an individual to operate, it might be easier to decide the kind of home business that would best suit her. These assessments may be available at a local library, community center, college, or small business administration (SBA) center.

With imagination and talent, a hobby can become a source of income. Here are some areas of interest most common among the SAHMs we surveyed—and the businesses that have emerged from them:[3]

Animals

pet grooming
animal breeding
pet sitting
pet walking
cleaning pet yards
pet taxi service

Antiquing

refurbishing and resale
acquisition and resale
consignment sales
eBay sales
bird-dog shopper for antique
  stores

Art

interior design
room/wall murals
painting sales/consignment
furniture manufacturing
  (specialty design)
manufacturing
gallery shows

Bargain Hunting

writing/topical articles/
  book sales
ebay sales business
saving enough to qualify for
  part-time income
consignment sales
perpetual garage sales/
  flea market sales

Cooking

cake decorating/sales
candy making
catering
caterer subcontractor
  (provides desserts or other
  specialty products)
meal-to-go for busy moms
cookie sales (guess where
  Mrs. Fields started)
cookbook author
specialty condiments
B&B cooking
menu planning

Children

childcare services
children's party planner
children's party bags
tutoring
preschool day trip provider
munchkin minder

Computers

Web site design
Web site maintenance
newsletter management
desktop publishing
legal transcriptionist
direct mail provider
personal organizer
travel planning
mail-order sales
online auctions
troubleshooting and repair
virtual assistant

Crafting

manufacturing and sales
consignment sales
lamps and lampshades
  specialties
craft fairs
interior design
scrapbooking provider
flea market sales
children's parties
school craft day provider
card making
  instruction

Electronics

media services
video demo services
electronic repairs

Entertaining

B&B
catering
party planner
party consultant

Finances

virtual assistant
daily money management
personal money management
senior citizen money
  management assistance
budget consultant
seminars on money
  management

Music

private, home instruction
tutoring
customized music videos
special events coordinator/
  consultant
reviewer

People

party planner
consultant
personal profile writer
freelance media relations
phone pollster

home-based sales
errand service

Photography

desktop media design
sales-direct (home studio
or on location)
brochures
video demo production
display design
consignment
photography instructor
photography writer

Physical Fitness

personal trainer
massage therapist
instructor
children's activity coordinator
consultant
fitness writer

Reading

book sales and resale
(eBay and Amazon.com)
editing
proofreading
writing
reviewer
researcher
consultant
tutoring

Selling

eBay and Internet sales
multi-level marketing sales

mail-order sales
network marketing
phone sales
catalog sales

Shopping/Buying

personal shopper
buy and sell (consignment
or Internet)
grocery personal shopper
virtual assistant

Scrapbooking

design
scrapbook services
scrapbook material sales
in-home classes

Sewing

alterations
repairs
custom sewing
costumes
design
instruction
interior design

Speaking

public speaking
women's conferences
speaking coach
instruction
consulting
seminars

Teaching

tutoring
home class instruction
education consultant
education writer

Tutoring

math
reading
music
English
language

science

Writing

newspaper freelancer
magazine articles
church or school newsletters
books
editor
desktop publishing
Web site content
writers conference faculty
online writer

Kinds of Businesses

The next action is to understand the three different kinds of businesses and their classifications:

Service business

This is the easiest kind of business to set up and usually requires the smallest initial investment and the simplest bookkeeping. It also tends to be an easy kind of business to run from home. According to Bernard C. Kamoroff, CPA and author of *Small Time Operator,* a service business also may require some experience and is more likely to be subject to state licenses and regulations. He says, "If you do something well—fixing things, painting or decorating, writing or editing, cutting hair, fixing or programming computers— these are but a few possibilities for your own service business. And if you are good at something, you might consider teaching those skills to others. Be imaginative. Don't ignore your own resources."[4]

Sales Business

Sales can take many forms—from retail or wholesale to storefront, mail order, direct sales, or network marketing. There are also consignment sales and Internet sales. Bookkeeping tends to be more complex, depending upon the kind of sales you offer. A sales business tends to be more flexible than a service business and offers more flexible hours. In sales whenever interests change, the sales business can change with them.

There might be a need to carry inventory, which could require a start-up cost for supplies and materials. Tax laws, credit card services, and banking issues are more complicated in a sales-based business.

Manufacturing

For the majority of homemade businesses manufacturing means crafts: jewelry, leather, clothing, pottery, furniture, home décor, etc. Crafts offer an opportunity for the craftsperson to do what she enjoys and get paid for it. The key is to offer a product others enjoy. An ugly seashell necklace may have been fulfilling to make, but if no one buys it, there isn't a business.

6 FINDING Your Dream Business

In 2005 almost 600,000 businesses opened; by 2008 the Small Business Administration expects only half of those will be in existence. This doesn't mean business failure; it just means only half of them stick around. To maximize a business proposition, consider the following steps:

1 **STEP ONE: Can You Hack It?**—Jane Pollack, the author of *Soul Proprietor*, wrote "The most necessary skill is the ability to show up."[5] This businesswoman took an egg-decorating passion and made it into a successful business. But don't confuse passion with talent—both are needed to start a legitimate homemade business. So is the ability to handle bookkeeping, time management, marketing, and more.

Isolation and rejection are often early business companions. The successful entrepreneur will need to take these undesirable partners by the hand and learn how to walk alongside them for a season. The client hates the way the scrapbook turned out; the cake wasn't the right flavor; the desktop project took so much time the profit was 50 cents an hour. All these come with establishing a home business. The SAHM needs to consider whether this is a good choice for her personality and her family.

2 **STEP TWO: Focus on What People Need**—A successful small-business or home-business owner targets what people need; often that aligns with what she needs herself. My family had a financial need I wanted to help meet while staying home with the babies.

When I started "Shop, Save, and Share Seminars," it was a tiny operation making no profits for three years. It targeted a financial need among stay-at-home moms and those trying to get out of debt. Our kids were two, four, six, eight, and ten years old at the time. Nine years later, it has grown up into Ellie Kay and Company, LLC, making significant profits that benefit the Kay Education Fund (smile intended) as well as several nonprofit organizations.

I have several employees, including my right hand, Wendy Wendler, who is the business manager. A team works hard for me: a literary agent, spokesperson agent, publicist, personal assistants for travel (I only use one at a time, depending upon who is available), a stylist, and a professional cleaner.

Among my other employees are the "Kay Kids" who perform: direct mail services, Internet sales, PowerPoint design, media relations, tape duplication, media kit marketing, on-site sales, personal assistant duties, postal metering, public relations coordination, and anything else I can think up to keep them gainfully employed and feeling part of the business team. I believe the most successful homemade businesses are those that incorporate the entire family —if the kids don't work in the business, they are at least supportive of it and understand why mom is doing this.

The point is: I started teaching a few coupon seminars because I had a business background, enjoyed public speaking, and wanted to help other moms learn to stretch their food dollars. This cottage industry has always been home centered, and it grew to the point that it may fund five children's college educations while teaching them a work ethic and providing a valuable service.

3 **STEP THREE: Test the Business Idea First**—Your mom may love your chocolate truffles, but that doesn't mean you can sell enough of them to qualify as a homemade business. It might cost more, in terms of time and supplies, than it is worth. It's critical for the future small business owner to test the idea in a sample market. One way is to get last year's phone book. Go through the Yellow Pages and call similar businesses to see if they are still in existence. This gives you an idea of whether the goods or services are viable for the community. Invest the time and energy in research. Go to the SBA (Small Business Administration's) Service Corp of Retired Executives for more research and help from local business development centers and networking groups. For example, if a mom decides she wants to launch a freelance writing career, it would be a good idea to attend a local writers' workshop or writers' group to see how many are turning a profit and how they are making it work.

4 **STEP FOUR: Stay in Touch with Trends**—The party planner needs to know what kids like, the photographer needs to have an eye for what the marketplace wants, and the personal shopper needs a constant fashion update to remain viable. Keep in mind that baby boomers want a scaled-down version of what is popular among adults for their kids. Women in their fifties want style that is new and fresh while in keeping with their lifestyle. Editors want writers who know what readers are demanding. Desktop publisher clients want materials that are cutting edge. A virtual personal assistant was unheard of a decade ago, but now busy working moms and corporate execs want someone to see their household bills are paid and their gardeners get their checks. By keeping up with trends, you can capitalize on the needs in the marketplace and create the maximum return for a minimum time investment.

5 **STEP FIVE: Consider Servicing Established Businesses**—In times of layoffs often the first people let go are those who provide peripheral services: IT, benefits, and even human resources. Many of these can be outsourced to an independent contractor. Some companies hire non-benefits-earning consultants to replace them, and these consultants work from home. With the right skills and an eye toward market trends, a savvy small-business owner can start servicing those companies.

6 **STEP SIX: The Family Council**—Once a SAHM has taken the necessary steps to have enough information, it's time to have a family council meeting—first with a spouse, then with the family. During this meeting, it's important for all sides of the issue to be discussed. A man might see advantages and disadvantages that his wife may not see, and at other times a man's understanding may be limited until he sees his wife's perspective. Start by considering three different kinds of homemade businesses; discuss the pros and cons of each as well as start-up costs, the realistic (don't fudge here) time commitment, and the realistic (*really* don't fudge here) projected net income (gross minus costs).

Once you have gone through the next section (Independent vs. Interdependent Businesses), fill out the Homemade Business Plan chart (figure 10.1) and discuss it.

Independent vs. Interdependent Businesses

Homemade businesses have something in common: they are all owned by independent small-business owners. This chapter will only address sole-proprietorship businesses (one owner), not partnerships or corporations. Many sole-proprietorship businesses are independent contractors who file their own taxes but have another employer such as a DSC (Direct Sales Company) or MLM (Multi-Level Marketing) associate.

There's a huge difference between manufacturing jewelry independently versus signing on as a jeweler with Premier Designs. This next section will help determine the difference between coming in under another business as an independent contractor and forging a new business.

When it comes to selling a product or service under another company while retaining a sole proprietorship status, it's more important than ever to do the market research. These companies identify themselves with different terms—some are called MLM or

DSC. Many of these offer products (such as bakeware, toys, or jewelry), sold through home parties. Consultants can sign up other consultants for the company and gain a portion of their profits as well. This usually holds true for three levels of consultants. This is why it is sometimes referred to as tri-level marketing.

Here are a few items to research when choosing a DSC, along with questions to help you make an informed decision:

—What are the up-front start-up costs (application fees, joining fees, authorization fees, etc.)?

—What down payment is required?

—What are the average gross profits of consultants?

—What are the minimum monthly or annual sales required?

—What are the minimum number of home shows required each month?

—How much inventory is needed?

—How much does the inventory cost to start up the business?

—What is the hostess plan? (free merchandise, bonus incentives, etc.)

—Does the consultant have to package and ship orders or does the DSC company?

—What is the customer shipping and handling fee?

—Are you paid up front?

—Does the consultant have to handle state tax issues or does the DSC company?

—What are the benefits of or opportunities for leadership in the next levels?

—What percentage of retail price does the consultant earn?

—What percentage of generations or downlines (people the consultant signs up to work for the DSC company) do the consultants get?

—How many downline generations are paid?

—Do you have to sign a certain number of downline consultants before you get a percentage?

—Does the DSC company print, track, and report downline activity, or is it up to the consultant to get this information directly?

—Can downline members break away or get promoted from under you?

—Do you have to cover specific territories?

—Are you required to fill out sales reports or call-ins?

—Does the DSC company have corporate debt or do they operate debt free?

—Is the DSC listed with the Better Business Bureau? (Conduct your own search at www.bbb.org.)

—Are they members of the Direct Selling Association? (Conduct your own search at www.dsa.org.)

Homemade Business Plan chart (Figure 10.1)					
Type of Business	Pros	Cons	Start-up Costs	Weekly Time Commitment	Projected Net Income
Business Option #1					
Business Option #2					
Business Option #3					
Business Option #4					

Tax Tips for the Grown-Up Homemade Business*

SEPs

Once a home business starts making money, it's time to consider setting up a Self Employment Pension plan where the business owner can contribute up to 25 percent of her compensation. This is different from an IRA in that you will need to include any employees over 21 years old who have worked for you for three of the last five years, including part-time employees if they have earned the minimum reportable income ($600.) The 25 percent "compensation" is your business profit reduced by the second Self-Employment Tax deduction, which is half the tax. Tax issues change from year to year and are more complicated than time and space will allow. For more information see Bernard Kamoroff's excellent book, *Small Time Operator.*

I set up my SEP without a CPA's help. It was easy—there were no IRS forms to file or administration fees to set it up. But my CPA tells me how much to fund it with each year when he prepares my taxes. If you're a sole proprietor, it's a good move since you only file this on yourself, and it will give you a full, portable retirement fund that you control.

LLCs

A decision to put your sole proprietorship under the structure of a Limited Liability Company is under the growing-up phase of your business, according to Kamoroff. He says, "LLCs are not as tightly regulated as limited partnerships and they offer greater liability protection." In researching the next step or growing-up step in my business (an LLC, S-Corp, LLP, etc.), I found an LLC offered many of the benefits, with few of the drawbacks of other incorporation options. I formed Ellie Kay and Company, LLC, by walking through the process with a business mentor. My CPA was surprised that I was able to do it so easily, but my mentor had already set up four such companies. Once again, this is a topic where you do the

*Also see "How to Find a Tax Preparer" in chapter 7.

research for your own small business and trust your CPA or accountant to advise you.

Once I did this and put it on all contracts, 1099 forms, stationery, invoices, etc., I found the credibility level jumped ten rungs. I wasn't perceived as some chickie-poo sorting coupons in her basement. Forming an LLC gave my trademarked brand and business additional credibility, as I'm perceived as the author, speaker, spokesperson, and media professional I've grown up to become.

Employees

Another significant tax question to put to your accountant has to do with employees. Most of us will have contract labor where we employ independent contractors, rather than traditional employees (where we would have paid Social Security, health insurance benefits, workers' comp, etc.).

If you pay someone $600 or more, you will need them to sign a W-9 form (download at www.irs.gov) with their personal info and Social Security or EIN (Employer Identification Number). You will have to file 1099-MISC forms for all your contractors at the end of the year and mail them by January 31. Then you'll file a 1096 with the IRS. All of this is info your CPA will handle or give you advice on.

Big point: Do *not* get in IRS trouble by paying an independent contractor $600 or more and then make the mistake of *not* filing a 1099/1096. If you pay an editor $600 to review your proposal or a Web site designer $700 to redo your site or a housekeeper $2,000 a year to clean your office, or your college son $800 a year to do your PowerPoint presentations—file the appropriate forms, or you're essentially paying under the table. If they don't have a Social Security number, don't hire them. Then, if you ever get nominated for a Supreme Court judge position, you won't have to worry about the investigators finding out that you paid your housekeeper on the sly because she was an illegal immigrant. Be above reproach and have a CPA or a small-business mentor show you where you're doing something stupid that you didn't know was against the law.

Advice from SAHM Homemade Business Owners

Email wendywendler@elliekay.com to receive contact info for any of the small business owners listed below.

"Treat your business like a business. Get up, get dressed, and go to work. You will not succeed by lying around until noon watching TV, allowing your time to be interrupted by visiting with friends or shopping, or having no schedule to keep you focused."

Jan McMinn, Colorado;
"The Window Seat," a custom sewing service

"There are so many opportunities available today because of technology. Find something you are interested in and make it into a business. Don't try to work at something you don't believe in yourself. Lastly, have fun with it."

Gina Horn, Texas; media booking

"My favorite aspect of my job is the flexibility and the ability to control my own calendar as well as the relationships I have made with other jewelers and the fact that I can take my job with me when we move (my husband is in the military). My family helps me in the business. My ten-year-old, Lauren, stamps catalogs and order forms with my name and address to earn money and assists me in shows. My five-year-old son, Jonathan, best understood how Mommy's jewelry shows benefit him when we bought a new play set for the backyard with jewelry show money."

Brenda Taylor, Texas; Premier Designs

"We needed health insurance for our home business, but it was too expensive. Then we went to www.ehealthinsurance. com and found we could afford it. Plus, we set up a tax-deferred HSA, which will help with our retirement."

Emily Grace, California

"Keep family a high priority so business doesn't dictate when you meet their needs or interfere with the quality of care they get."

Lori Hudson, Nebraska; Country Bunny Bath and Body

"Do something for your business every day (M–F), whether organizing your desk area and files, or making phone calls to customers (booking shows or making sure they received your latest flyer). Always be working toward a specific goal and verbalize that goal to others."

Gwen Christel, Nebraska; Longaberger Baskets

"My children have seen how Mom is more available with a home business. I have more money to give to church, and I have satisfaction in what I do and the product I sell. My advice to homemade business owners is to know your company, know your product, understand your market, get support from friends and family, be secure in what you do, have fun, and make it a priority that your business does not interfere with your family life."

Jan Johnson, Texas; Southern Living at Home (direct sales)

"Get a reality check. Don't fool yourself, because it's not easy. Owning your own business takes work, perseverance, and determination. To be successful you need thick skin at times and an attitude of 'I won't give up.' The rewards are amazing but you definitely earn them. . . . I am fortunate that the Mary Kay Company has a wonderful mentoring and support program. Just being able to talk to someone when I feel like I am going nowhere is a big help."

Karen Evenson, California; Mary Kay Cosmetics

"Operating a successful small business requires involvement from all the family. Each member should be included in the decision to get into business, because they will all be affected by it. Consider the way it will impact your involvement in school activities, church, and civic organizations."

Cheryl Shelton, Texas; S&P Enterprises (stock trading)

"I started freelancing after working in public relations at the seminary my husband and I were attending after we got married. I realized that at $5.50 an hour, I was working for peanuts writing about the seminary's new pool. Not my idea of fun! I also had a lifelong dream of writing books, so with my hubby's support, I quit my job and started freelancing. I figured I could sell one or two articles a month and make what I was making working 25 hours a week. And God was so good! I began making money that first month, and though I've had ups and downs, I am absolutely *loving* being a mommy to two boys and working around their schedules. I wouldn't trade my job for anything! I have had three books and hundreds of articles published, and I speak regularly to women's groups."

Dena Dyer, Texas; Grace Notes (author/speaker)

"My home-based business has given me a once-in-a-lifetime opportunity of financial and time freedom and the chance to give others the gift of doing the same. Above all, having my own business has also blessed me with an opportunity to grow personally."

Trissina Laube, California;
Independant Counsultant for Arbonne International

Proverbs 22:7 says, "The rich rules over the poor and the borrower is servant to the lender."

HOW TO FINISH Great, No Matter Where You Start

We attended the wedding of a young man who worked for Bob, and it was an experience I'll never forget. The young man's fiancé made him leave the Air Force Academy to marry her. (You can't be married and attend the academy.) So he left his dream of becoming an officer for his new chief of staff. But it was only an omen of things to come.

I'll never forget how uncomfortable I was when "Carlos" told his friends at the wedding, "Just don't say anything to Maria. Don't look at her and don't talk to her—or she might get mad!"

By the time we got seated in the church, the processional was about to begin. There were twelve bridal attendants and the same number of groomsmen. It was a huge wedding with elaborate flowers, decorations, and a spectacular reception. There was only one thing missing. A happy bride.

There was a bride, but she was far from happy. Apparently someone looked at her or talked to her.

In their tradition the bride and groom walked the aisle together in the processional. So Carlos entered the church with Maria on his arm. They walked step . . . together, step . . . together, all the way up the aisle. You could see her flushed face even under the veil. She grabbed Carlos's arm and dug her nails into his sleeve. She had a word to speak at every step.

Step . . . together.

"Porque tu amiga me mira de esa forma?"

Step . . . together.

"Estoy muy irritada, porque debias de haber preguntado antes de invitarla."

Step . . . together.

"Te arrepentiras de haberlo hecho?"

Yep. For those of you who aren't fluent in Spanish, the translation was: Someone looked at the bride wrong, the groom was in deep trouble, and she was making sure he knew it. I half-suspected his friends were rooting for him to become the "Runaway Groom."

This couple was beginning a new phase of life together, and they were already out of step. What should have been a grand fiesta was starting to look like many lean years of famine.

****

There are some couples who make a similar mistake when it comes to financial matters of prime importance. When you embark on a new phase of life called *half-price living*, it's important to have a firm foundation and be on the same team as a couple and as a family. It's a little like a solid table with four good legs. The legs to living on one income are family, friends, finances—and faith. We've already discussed the first three elements, so here we'll tap into the most critical part of the human experience. Here are some key principles families need to understand to make sure their table stays firmly planted and doesn't topple over.

Stewardship

Stewardship is acknowledging that God owns it all. Mankind manages the resources God has given. If we believe this, every financial decision has spiritual implications. Good stewards want to do a good job with the gifts, talents, and financial resources they are given. Someone can pretend they're in debt when they're not or pretend they are loaded when they're in debt, but no one can fake good financial stewardship—it's all written in their checkbook.

Cynthia from Georgia was a civil-service worker only three months away from retaining her achieved rank when her daughter was born. She said, "I saw those big blue eyes and knew I would not be able to leave her, even for only three months. I have been a stay-at-home mom now for fifteen years (with four children). I have always said anyone can live on one income; it is what you choose to invest in and be a steward of that matters. I choose to invest in the lives of my children and my husband."

Contentment

Have you ever been around someone who isn't happy no matter what? I remember when we lived in gorgeous Colorado Springs —truly God's country. One of the other military wives and I were talking about the fact that we had both just moved there and I said, "Isn't this an incredibly beautiful part of the world with Pike's Peak, the evergreens, and the aspens?"

She shrugged. "Not really, I don't think it's all that great. I really liked Virginia." All I could think was that this woman must be loads of fun to live with if she can't find any reason to be content with Colorado. I mean, Colorado's Rocky Mountain Chocolate Factory should do it, if nothing else. Paul wrote, "Not that I speak from want, for I have learned to be content in whatever circumstances I am." (Philippians 4:11). I believe contentment is a choice; the sooner we choose to be content in money matters, the sooner we'll be a lot happier—and a lot easier to live with.

Judy, a grandmother who lives in Palmdale, says sometimes she fights the idea of contentment when it comes to staying home instead of working outside the home. "When I hear stories of what other women are doing in the workplace and I let pressure from these stories make me feel like I haven't accomplished or added much, then I can get discontent. But I always remind myself of what I was able to be and do for my family by staying home with them. I remember that I could volunteer in important areas to me—the classroom, among the poor, at the food pantry, and in politics, then I choose to be content."

Tithing

All the major financial experts from David Bach, to Suze Orman and Dave Ramsey, to Howard Dayton and Ron Blue—advocate the idea of the tithe. The literal translation of this is "the tenth" or that portion of our income. Certain principles just work, and giving a tenth is a foundational principle in sound financial stewardship.

Dena, a former actress from Grapevine, Texas, wrote, "One thing I'm glad my hubby and I have been on the same page about: we've always tithed, no matter how tight things were. When we were first married, we were both in seminary and working part time. We lived on $1,000 a month. Now we make a lot more than that—but we have two kids, so we could always spend more than we make. With God's provision and supportive parents on both sides, we have never lacked for anything. I believe that's partly because we have always given at least 10 percent, at times 15 percent, to our church and other nonprofit organizations."

Provision

Kay from Redondo Beach, a young mom with an Ivy League degree, says, "I'm teaching our son that having mom at home is more important than having more material wealth. Ultimately, we're really learning how God always provides for our needs." She left her teaching job to stay home and go into ministry full time with her husband. They see a constant provision for all their needs.

Pam from San Diego said their early years were tight; they could barely pay the rent and basic bills. "But when it came to paying the extras—like when the tires needed to be replaced, or the refrigerator broke, or the car died, we were always praying for a miracle—once we went without a car for months while we prayed. God did provide—two bikes—and we got in super shape. Then someone in our church offered us a car that was awesome. All we had to pay for was a brake job, so we got a car for $65. Four times in our early marriage God either gave us cars or money from someone to help pay for a car."

These families illustrate the principle that there is joy in seeing God provide for your needs.

Abundance

"And I will bless those who bless you, and the one who curses you I will curse. And in you all the families of the earth shall be blessed" (Genesis 12:3). The abundance principle goes hand in hand with the provision principle—they are sisters. God never blesses you abundantly for you to keep it to yourself. He blesses you so you can be a blessing to others.

Kris from New Mexico was willing to live on one income to serve as a volunteer to start a ministry to the homeless. All her abundance went into the lives of others. She says, "I've never felt unfulfilled. I'll never have Social Security or a credit history, but I must say I never have trouble sleeping—I rest my head every night in God's abundant love and fulfillment."

Fellowship

A boy who was scared of the dark told his mom it wasn't enough that God was with him in the scary room. He explained, "I want God with skin on!" That's at the heart of basic fellowship.

Suzanne, a former Air Force engineer who left her job to stay home, wrote, "Ellie, I think it's important that a woman at home has other friends who stay at home and also live off one income. A stay-at-home mom needs friends and plenty of adult communication throughout the day while her husband is at work. [If] you have other friends who live off of one income . . . you are not trying to keep up with the Joneses (a two-income family) as you and your children socialize."

It's also important to plug into a *group* that will help develop the financial attitudes that are consistent with a stewardship lifestyle. One such spiritually based group is Crown Financial Ministries (www.crown.org). This site offers a list of study groups that help participants learn to manage money from a spiritual perspective. (It doesn't matter if you're great or terrible with money.)

Encouragement

There are two sides to the encouraging coin. The first is the feel-good encouragement that comes from observing the lives of people who have overcome financial hardships. However, the other side of encouragement has to do with kindly and gently telling the truth in love. If we can't make rent one month and our friend comes over and sees the new Bose surround-sound system we just bought—she's going to encourage us to get our priorities straight. Everyone needs friends who will give both sides of encouragement.

My friend Madeline from Colorado has been a major encourager to me. She and I may not speak for months, but then she'll call and say, "I just had to tell you I was praying for you and thinking of you." Then she speaks the most wonderful promises into my life. But she's also been able to speak words of caution to me and even call me on the carpet. All of this is because we have the relationship that speaks both kinds of encouragement—each kind motivated by love and the others' greater good.

Wisdom

"But in abundance of counselors there is victory," says Proverbs 11:14. This doesn't mean it's a good idea to run from one person to another—gathering their ideas as if taking a poll on how a problem should be resolved. Rather, in this context it encourages us to develop a relationship with another couple who shares mutual respect and can give solid advice. It doesn't mean every bit of advice is followed, because no one has all the answers, but it's important to ask.

Morgan, a former actress, gives this sage advice to new one-income moms, "Prepare mentally, and remember why you're doing it. For us it was so I could be a full-time mom. So when doubt or fear crept in (or even materialism), I reminded myself that the reason for staying home far outweighed the extra paycheck. Practically speaking, before you go to one paycheck look at how you spend money on stuff you really don't need. Learn to bargain hunt. Have fun looking for the best deals. Don't buy anything if it's not on sale. Look for ways to save five or ten dollars. I even get excited when I find a way to save one dollar. Also, if at all possible, pay off some debt before leaving work; this is a huge help."

Freedom from Debt

Proverbs 22:7 says, "The rich rules over the poor, and the borrower becomes the lender's slave." And Romans 13:8 says, "Owe nothing to anyone except to love one another."

Here are some reasons to lose the debt.

—Debt puts your marriage at risk, as it's the number one reason cited in divorce.

—Debt makes you servant to the lender.

—Debt borrows from your future.

—Debt borrows on your children's future.

—Debt keeps you from seeing the joy of God's provision.

—Debt hinders your ability to share abundantly with others.

—Debt erodes resources through high-interest payments.

—Debt sets a poor example for your children.

Savings

The spiritual principle of saving ties in with the principles of wisdom, diligence, and freedom from debt. Someone who saves or invests money is usually wise, and this often requires diligence. Plus, if people have debt, their money would have to go toward payments rather than toward a savings account. Proverbs 13:11 says, "Wealth obtained by fraud dwindles, but the one who gathers by labor increases it."

One of the most frequently repeated statements in our one-income-living survey was that if these women had a do-over before living on one income, they would have put more into savings. I often hear from women who want to live on one income but do not have savings (rather, they have major debt), which makes it impossible.

Christin from New York wrote,

> I would like to live on one income so I would not have the mental burden of providing financially for my family. Though I love the company I work for and the people I work with, I would love being at home more.
>
> I would like to be able to focus on the emotional, physical, and spiritual needs of my spouse and children. Things are going on inside my children's heads that I cannot deal with due to time constraints. I have a large family and don't have enough one-on-one time with anyone in my family.
>
> I would also like to be able to take care of my home better, to manage it more efficiently so that it would run more smoothly and things could be less stressful. With two parents working outside the home, it is difficult to take care of the housekeeping and shopping and clutter like it needs to be taken care of. I perform household tasks, but I don't do things as well as I would like to. Sometimes things just get half-way done! . . .
>
> But if I were to try and even think about living on one income, I'd need at least six months' worth of my salary in the bank, and I can't see that happening anytime soon.

Personal Renewal

It's hard to take care of money issues, financial woes, or one-income prospects if there are physical health limitations. It's hard to isolate a part of a human being, for example, the spiritual life, and call it independent, because it is interdependent upon other areas. The need for personal renewal is one that affects the entire person: physically, emotionally, mentally, and spiritually. So if the focus is only on spiritual life to the exclusion of the other aspects, the point of personal renewal is missed. Let's take a look at each of these elements necessary for vibrant personal health, and therefore financial health.

Pam, a mother of three boys, said, "Once a year, I get my favorite study books, my Bible, music, a beach towel, snacks, water, and a chair, and I spend the day at the beach completely alone. I spend that time for personal renewal and to hear from God about the upcoming year. I find this exercise to be critical to my spiritual life."

Physical

I once heard a well-known conservative preach against the use of birth control. When he was asked about the effects on the health of a woman who has eight children in ten years and the subsequent weight gain, he responded, "Well, she can just have all her children; then when she's through she can go on a crash diet and lose eighty pounds!" He was serious.

Physical well-being is, in some ways, a reflection of a person's spiritual status. If the body is the temple of the Holy Spirit, it ought to be well cared for. By exercising, eating healthy foods, and managing stress, a woman is better able to serve others and meet their spiritual needs.

I have to work out to keep my energy level up. I've always done this—even when the five kids were seven and under. I'd put two children in the double stroller, one would be on his bicycle, the toddler would be strapped on my backpack, and the newborn in swaddling clothes across my chest. I carried forty pounds of children and pushed another eighty pounds of them; but by golly, I got my workout!

Suzanne from Las Vegas says, "I enjoy living on one income and working out at the health club because I can help others get physically fit. I am passionate about health and fitness, and I am able to positively influence the lives of others, which is rewarding."

Emotional

This part of a person blends into the social aspects of our identity. Healthy friendships with my girlfriends are some of the greatest things I can do for my emotional health. While Bob is my best friend, he's not a woman (which I appreciate greatly). And while my children are fun to talk to, they aren't equipped to handle my emotional baggage—especially those related to money matters. When we are emotionally healthy, we are less likely to participate in impulse buying, foolish money decisions, and unwise purchases.

I need the outlet of these friendships in which I can vent, laugh, and be encouraged. I also stop to *listen* to my girlfriends when they need to talk. Lasting friendships are about giving and taking, and we need both.

Speaking of giving . . . When I'm going through a personal crisis or feeling depressed, one of the best things I can do is to reach out to others. Sometimes when we help a friend through her problems we forget our own. I also volunteer at the homeless shelter. Over the years I've done all kinds of acts of service. It keeps me emotionally healthy to forget my problems for a while and reach out to help someone else.

Mental

When I went to Colorado Christian University to get a degree in the management of human resources, little did I know I would one day be managing *so many* little human resources!

Many stay-at-home-moms who are with children during the day find it too easy to fall into the rut of neglecting this part of themselves. But remaining healthy mentally is important to who a mom is in the long run—and it's especially important when it comes to knowing the latest ways to save money, invest, and teach kids about finances.

In my CCU class there was a lady named Madeline who was seventy years old. She'd never finished her degree and wanted to do it—so she did. She was also the author of two books, and I thought that was the coolest thing ever. I think of Madeline every now and then, and she is an inspiration to me still!

Reading, using the imagination to dream dreams and problem solve, planning for the future, engaging in creative writing, developing new talents, and learning new skills are all part of developing the mind.

Brideshead Revisited

This brings us back to our story from the beginning of this chapter where the wife established her supremacy while walking down the aisle to get married. There is a critical balance in the spiritual life, where the wife appreciates her husband's input but she is never made to feel subservient in the relationship. One person has to be responsible for the final decision, but it should be a joint effort in the process. This is especially true when it comes to financial matters. It is sometimes easier for husbands and wives to agree on how many children to have rather than how the money will be spent. But our spiritual lives need to become a priority to build the firm financial foundation necessary in *half-price living.*

Don't let time pressures or money woes or financial distractions erode your family's spiritual lives. Your spiritual bonds are some of the most intimate aspects of your relationship. Building a firm spiritual foundation requires a lot of effort and energy, but your family is worth it.

Thirty Days to a Wiser You

The wisdom literature of the Psalms and Proverbs is a great text to study about finances. In fact, there is more about the topic of money than any other topic in those books. Try reading the following wisdom literature every month for two months and see if you aren't the wiser for the effort:

Day 1—Read Proverbs 1, Psalms, 1, 31, 61, 91, and 121.

Day 2—Read Proverbs 2, Psalms, 2, 32, 62, 92, and 122.

Days 3–28—Continue reading the Proverb chapter that relates to the day of the month and every thirtieth Psalm that relates to the day of the month (as in Days 1 and 2).

Day 29—Read Proverbs 29, Psalms 29, 59, 89 (skip Psalm 119), and 149

Day 30—Read Proverbs 30, Psalms 30, 60, 90, 120, and 150.

Day 31—Read Proverbs 31 and Psalm 119.

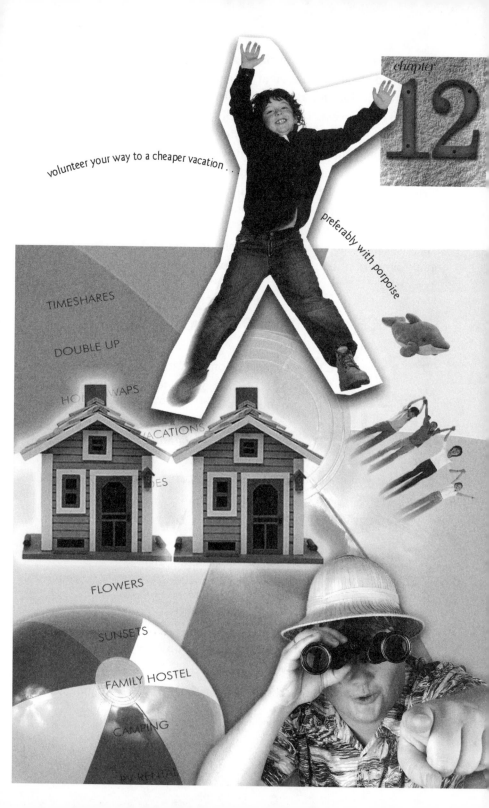

chapter 12

volunteer your way to a cheaper vacation . . .

preferably with porpoise

TIMESHARES

DOUBLE UP

HOME SWAPS

VACATIONS

FLOWERS

SUNSETS

FAMILY HOSTEL

CAMPING

HOW TO RESTRUCTURE
Vacations and Build Memories

"Steph! Jimmy! Be sure to pack your CD players! Misty, don't forget your favorite slippers!" my friend Annie called as her kids were packing for a road trip.

The children were excited about taking their first vacation in a long time as they prepared to visit a luxury seacoast community in Southern California where Don's parents lived. This community is known for the porpoise that often frolicked along the coastline. They rented the house next door so they could visit the grandparents yet retain privacy for special family bonding moments. Little did they know how much bonding they would do after they arrived.

The first day went well. The kids explored the beach searching for the porpoise, and they spent time with their grandparents. Don got in some exercise, and Annie caught up on her reading. But the next morning, the tide began to change.

The teenagers were camped out in a large room downstairs while their parents were in the upstairs master bedroom. The youngest, Misty, was the first to wake up to a strange smell. She groggily asked her older brother as she wrinkled her nose, "Jimmy, did you take a shower last night?"

"Yes, I showered." He looked around the room in disgust. "Yuck! It isn't me!" Sitting up in his sleeping bag, he shook his older sister awake.

"Hey, Steph, I think your couch has a problem; it's smelling up the whole room!"

Enlisting the help of their parents, the whole family went on a search for the source of the increasingly disgusting odor. Their quest took them to the basement door. When they opened it, the pungent odor threatened to overtake them and left no doubt as to the source. The five vacationers ran up the stairs and out the door shrieking: "SKUNK!"

The smell blasted through the vents and blanketed the house. The family's clothing, jackets, and sleeping bags were saturated. The "porpoise" of the vacation was soon forgotten as the family learned a new meaning to the old phrase, "Our vacation stank!"

****

There is another way vacations can stink—when expenses decay your vacation budget until there's nothing left but a pile of credit card receipts. There *is* a way to have a memory-making getaway that doesn't add to your debt—if you purpose to make your vacation worthwhile.

Here are four ways to take a holiday break without breaking the bank:

Share Your Time with Time-Shares

Debby May and her husband, Steve, had been married twenty-five years and only taken two family vacations. They would get a little bit ahead financially, and then something would happen to crack their vacation savings nest egg—a job loss, unexpected medical bills, or auto repairs. Then they heard about a time-share presentation offered by Hilton Grand Vacations Clubs in Las Vegas, a four-hour drive from their home.

The Mays stayed at a posh resort hotel for $50 per night and were given $100 in chips, which rather than gamble with, they immediately cashed in. Since the suites had cooking facilities, they inexpensively covered most of their meals. They spent two hours on the tour and time-share presentation, which they declined to purchase. The total cost for this vacation was $85 in gas and $105 for food. The total, after turning in the $100 chips, was only $90. Steve and Debby were pleased with their holiday fun and said they would do it again.

If you choose to pursue this idea, be sure you are able to say no to a sales pitch. Before you book, ask questions about the introductory offer: How many nights does the fee cover? Are children allowed? Can you use all the facilities free (parking, pool, gym, Internet)?

Another option is to share another family's regular time-share. Some couples get several weeks on their ownership programs each year; sometimes they can't take the time off work, or they give the week away to another family member. The Howe family, for example, considers this a "tithe" off their financial resources.

Most time-share owners pay an average of $250 for the week they are at the facility. If you can't find a solo time-share, consider sharing space with a friend or family member's time-share. For example, there might be a family in your neighborhood, church, work, or community who is willing to split that fee and share the space. Or you could offer to pay the entire week of fees because $250 is still an inexpensive rate for a week of fun at a nice resort.

What if you have a time-share and want to sell it? Go to this link to find information on how to do that: http://homebuying.about.com/cs/timeshareresales/a/sell_timeshare.htm.

Double Up Anywhere Anytime

If you have friends you like *a lot* and think your friendship can survive the test of a family vacation, double up with that family and cut your lodging bill in half. The Greaves family wrote me about how they did this with the Morton family and enjoyed it so much that they made it an every-other-year tradition. The normal price of a week-long mountain cabin rental with three bedrooms was $900. "We made sure we knew all the costs ahead and there were no financial surprises," says Loretta Greaves. Each family paid $450 and their own gas for a destination that might not have been available to them otherwise. "We really couldn't swing nearly $1,000 for the week on my pastor's salary, but we could afford half that amount, and we've truly enjoyed our time off," said Mike Morton.

You don't have to rent a cabin to double up with another family. There are many kinds of rentals listed at www.findrental.com. Suite hotels that offer extra rooms are also an option, such as the ones found at www.orbitz.com or www.cheaprooms.com. For those who love the great outdoors, sharing campsite fees or RV rentals can split the price of a camping adventure. At www.rvrental.com we found rentals across the country that ranged from $117 to $385 per day. Other charges to consider may be hospitality kits, kitchen kits, and/or emergency road kits. Cleaning fees will apply if the RV is not returned in the condition in which it was rented.

Home Swaps: Ticket for Savings

Swapping homes is an idea that has been around a long time but is gaining popularity due to e-mail and an ever-increasing number of Web-based exchange services such as www.homelink.org, www.intervac.org, and www.homeexchange.com. Many swappers like the ease of listing their homes and entertaining offers from places they never considered visiting. The other advantage is that instead of leaving your own empty house as burglar bait, you have the place occupied while you're away.

Most of these exchange services charge $30 to $110 per year. If the listed date for a specific location isn't within your time frame, you can e-mail swappers from that destination and ask if they could be flexible with their dates.

The key question is: Is it safe to turn over your home to someone else? But home swappers (and exchange services) report remarkably few problems. According to Dan Akst, a writer for MSN Money, "Home exchangers tend to be prosperous, mature, well-educated professionals—not the types most likely to trash your home."

This alternative is especially attractive to families with children, for whom hotel stays and lots of restaurant meals are expensive and not often enjoyable. One strategy is to swap with families who also have children, thereby adopting a kid-friendly home. Another added benefit is that the kids enjoy playing with all those strange new toys.

The main expense you will have will be the travel cost to your destination. For the best airfares, go to www.cheaptickets.com, www.expedia.com, www.orbitz.com, or www.travelocity.com. Once you find the cheapest fare, open a second Internet window and immediately compare the same flight with the carrier's direct site—sometimes you can save as much as $50 per ticket off of the best price.

Most swappers prefer to begin with an exchange near home to get their feet wet before they swap with a family in Italy or Bora Bora. A family of four in New York purchasing advance-fare tickets at $229 each could pay the $85 swap fee and visit Paris for only $991.

Best advice for home swappers: Leave instructions or a user manual for your home, check with your insurance company to make sure the new family is covered, and don't expect the Taj Mahal.

Volunteer Your Way to a Cheaper Vacation (Preferably—with Porpoise)

Mac and Dina Thompson discovered their favorite family vacation spot when they had an ample budget for family fun. They went to a Christian campground in Colorado and fell in love with the staff, landscape, and activities. They also caught the vision of how combining ministry with vacation can help teach their kids the concept of servant missions.

When Mac decided to go to law school and start a second career in his forties, they found their vacation budget reduced. They opted to go back to the campground as staff for a week. While their workload was increased, they had plenty of family time with a ministry emphasis. Mac said, "We decided to volunteer to teach our children the benefits of servant missions and *not* for the benefit of a low-cost vacation—that is a serendipitous blessing."

Instead of paying $1,000 for the week (which is still a bargain for paid guests), they had a working vacation for free. Not all campgrounds offer this kind of a trade-off, but if your family enjoys this environment, contact a local retreat center or campground. Go to www.acacamps.org for the American Camp Association or try www.google.com and enter your state and "Christian Campground" to find a location near you.

Not all vacation packages are faith-based; some are education-based. At www.journeysforfamilies.travel there are trips that match families with learning vacations around the world, while Elder-hostel at www.elderhostel.com offers those 55 and older up to 10,000 options starting at as little as $556 for a six-day photography workshop in Massachusetts.

Wilderness Volunteers, www.wildernessvolunteers.org, is a non-profit organization created in 1997 that offers people of any age a chance to help maintain U.S. national parks, forests, and wilderness areas. Projects include everything from trail maintenance to revegetation. Participants provide their own camping gear and share campsite chores. Most Wilderness Volunteer trips last a week and cost around $219.

No matter what your vacation budget is, it's important to take time off from the real world to create meaningful time for your marriage and family. In years to come, you may not recall the price of the condominium or quality of the room service. But you will remember those moments with the people you love—because they are *priceless*.

How to Woo the One You Love

It can be difficult to cultivate "romance moments" with your spouse while on vacation with the kids. But couple moments can happen if you grab them where you can. Here are some ways for you to connect in your marriage without disconnecting from the family.

Beach Time—When playing in the waves, take time to snuggle your mate in the water.

Balcony Dates—Try to select a room with a view; while the kids are asleep or watching a movie, have coffee on the veranda under the stars.

Flowers Anyone?—Surprise your mate with a bouquet from a street vendor.

Sunsets—Check out the time of sunset at www.weatherchannel.com, and schedule dinner at a local restaurant, asking for a table with a view.

Gifts—Before your vacation, wrap a few inexpensive, meaningful gifts for your mate. Place one on his/her pillow each night.

Touch—Meaningful touch can often get lost in the rapid pace of life. Grab your spouse's hand and give him a kiss under the moonlight.

Carriage Ride—Take advantage of the romantic element in family activities. Let your kids ride in the front of a carriage while you snuggle in the back.

Reflection Time—Schedule a date at the end of each day to share what you felt was your "most romantic moment" and why. You may be surprised at what you learn about your mate.

. . . make a difference in the lives of others and train your children to do the same.

chapter

13

THE BENEFIT of Sharing and Stewardship

I met her at a writers' group meeting. We were both late, so we sat at one end of the table together. She was sixty-five years old with lovely silver hair, a dazzling, smooth-skinned smile, and a "fill the room" presence.

She is Jewish—I'm Protestant.

She is a liberal—I'm a conservative.

She's single—I'm married.

She's mostly a Democrat—I'm mostly a Republican.

She lives alone—I live with six people, three parakeets, and a pampered puppy.

She is old enough to be my mom—I was smart enough not to mention it.

We have nothing in common—and everything in common.

While I grew up in the cow town of Fort Worth, Texas, Yvonne was raised in privileged neighborhoods and grew up with the kids of Hollywood's rich and famous. Yvonne invited us to Seder and Hanukah. We invited her to Christmas and Easter.

On several Monday nights she took me into Beverly Hills to a classic film series at the Academy (as in the-Academy-Awards-Academy).

It was a thrill to sit in the famous theater with twelve-foot golden Oscars on either side of the stage. We watched the film on a full screen and listened to a panel of actors, directors, and writers from the fifties discuss their roles in the movies we screened.

Yvonne also introduced me to the 99-cent store, and I was "home." There was quality in these stores, unlike some of the junkie junk I found in dollar stores elsewhere. There were the items in the 99-cent store that I saw at other stores—and these were 75 percent off the retail price. I found our "Happy Plates" there (ceramic yellow plates with the happy eyes and mouth on them) and some gorgeous green-tinted martini-type glasses. I fill the hoity-toity glasses with sparkling apple cider (also purchased for 99 cents), and the kids pretend they're movie stars as they drink a toast to Miss Yvonne.

Besides our mutual appreciation of old movies, our love of the hunt for a bargain, and the fact that we are both authors—there's one other thing we have in common: We want to help other people in practical, tangible ways.

Yvonne had a friend whose mother was a part of a "Sewing Club" for forty years. Every week, the women got together when their kids were in school and their husbands were at work to chat and visit. Even though they never sewed a stitch, they maintained friendships there that lasted until death—over four decades.

Yvonne wanted to capture that sense of community, but sewing is a lost art in a modern age, and most schedules are so busy that a once-a-week commitment isn't going to happen. So she decided to form a "Sowing Club." The concept is that once a month ten women gather and each contribute $10 for items to be purchased at the 99-cent store (or other bargain places). Yvonne says, "There is so much need, and where do you start? Well, you can start at home. Ten dollars, by itself, isn't that much, but $100 when spent at a bargain store can make for a huge pile of donations."

A different, local nonprofit organization is targeted each month, and the group sorts and organizes donated items for delivery. While chatting and eating cookies around Yvonne's table, the gabby group forms an assembly line. Marilyn gets a washcloth and passes it to Joan, who puts in a small-sized shampoo and conditioner; she passes it to Chice, who puts in soap and a toiletry kit; she passes it to Chris, who adds a comb, then Emily adds a shower cap; and it ends up with me. Since I'm the creatively challenged one, I clumsily close the washcloth and put a colorful scrunchie and bow around the top. When I'm not looking, Yvonne straightens and fixes my work.

Besides the monetary donations, group members donate other items from home such as hotel mini-toiletries, food, clothing, toys, and books. One member, a musical artist, donated a dozen CDs. The artistic side of us is sewn into the fabric of our community as we place a tag on each bundle that says, "Bringing you . . . (only one of the following is on each card) Resolve, Joy, Inspiration, Hope. From the Sowing Club of the Antelope Valley."

I went on the delivery to the Women's Crisis Center and the homeless shelter. These places told us they are used to getting donations of much-worn (and often dirty) clothing and beat-up toys. Consequently, their eyes lit up when they saw that we had boxes of new items, wrapped happily with bows. At the homeless shelter we arrived during the weekly check-in time. There were dozens of people waiting outside with luggage, hoping a spot would open for them. Some of the residents helped us carry in the bounty. One of the men, a man in his thirties with a sad smile and pale blue eyes, said, "Why are you doing this? What church are you with?"

I smiled and placed my hand on his arm. "I'm not with a church; there's just a group of us who meet each month, and we call ourselves the 'Sowing Club.' It's a bunch of women who live in your town who want to help you find your feet and follow them home."

He stood there a moment, a box in his rough hands, looking into my face. Before he turned away, I saw—ever so briefly—that he was fighting back tears. As he carried in the box he said, "That's what I'd like to do. Find my feet. Find a way home."

The concept of our little club is spreading. There's been a feature in the local paper and interest expressed from one of the largest news stations in Los Angeles County. I went on an interview with this station, KTLA, to talk about cutting your food bill in half and had the opportunity to talk about donating some of those food items through a group like our club. Yvonne has had others try to make a donation to our group but she says, "No, we're not a formal nonprofit; there's just a small group of us who get together to do this. Why don't you start your own Sowing Club with your neighbors, coworkers, and friends?"

I wonder what could happen in our communities if people of similar backgrounds would get together and give resources to those in need in their own communities? If Sowing Clubs were to spring up all across the country, it could change the world—99 cents at a time.

I guess that's the thing I appreciate most about the Sowing Club. It's not a formal organization—not that there's anything wrong with structured nonprofit organizations. But sometimes people don't reach out to help others because they get bogged down in "what group do I join?" and "where is the best place to donate my money or items?" We can start in our own neighborhoods, just like Yvonne did.

****

Treating the Troops

While starting at home is a great idea, there are other people who try to make a difference around the world. One person at a time—or one cookie at a time—like Jeanette Cram.

Jeanette Cram is a certifiable crumb. You may have seen her on the *Martha Stewart Show* or read about her exploits in *Good Housekeeping*. But the first place to look for Jeanette is in her kitchen. She's known around the world as the cookie lady who has been baking homemade goodies for soldiers on the front line since the Gulf War in 1990, when a letter from a soldier read by then-President George H. W. Bush gave her the idea. Some 130,000 cookies later, she's still preheating the oven and measuring flour. Jeannette laughs and says, "Sometimes I get tired thinking about how big we've become—I must be out of my mind."

Everyday people, like Jeanette Cram, are making a huge difference in the lives of military men and women serving in the Middle East, and so can you.

Operation: Close to Home

Gladys Walker, the founder of "Have a Heart/Adopt A Soldier," had a son stationed in Afghanistan in 2002 and regularly sent him care packages. He asked her to send more so he could share with the guys who never got a letter in the mail. Gladys said, "The idea that these poor boys thought no one cared if they lived or died broke my heart. I knew we had to do something." The first month she sent twelve parcels. Now the organization has mailed over 3,600 care packages and continues to grow, staffed by volunteers. "I got a note from Donald Rumsfeld," exclaimed an amazed Gladys, "thanking me for what we are doing for the troops. That's not why I do it, but I'm still going to frame the note!"

The best place to begin is your own backyard. Ask friends from your neighborhood, church, or community for the names and addresses of family members and friends stationed overseas. There may be a friend of a son, daughter, father, or mother who has little contact from those in the United States. Informal groups can adopt a military member, sending notes and care packages regularly. When six months stretches into eighteen and the letters keep coming, they can be the primary lifeline of hope to a lonely soldier, sailor, or airman.

Operation: Courageous Character

When my husband, Bob, flew the F-117A fighter and was on long military deployments, he spent many days away from family and church fellowship. He said, "There were constant temptations and opportunities to compromise moral character." It was, and is, a constant struggle for soldiers to stay faithful to core values. Families can help cultivate this character by creating a Service Member Wish Book. Be creative in putting together these wishes; then mail the items to an adopted service member:

I wish for you . . . the courage to laugh with friends (a funny card, humor book or share a family anecdote).

I wish for you . . . the courage to redeem beauty for ashes (send something lovely created out of something unusual).

I wish for you . . . the courage to choose peace and tranquility (include a mood music CD with a note as to why your family likes the music).

I wish for you . . . the courage to cherish memories (a personalized family photo).

I wish for you . . . the courage to keep in touch (a phone card).

I wish for you . . . the courage to be wise (a favorite book).

I wish for you . . . the courage to be cool and fresh (mints).

Operation: Compassionate Kids

Kids can get involved in caring for others around the world as well. Approach a classroom teacher, Scout leader, or after-school club about the idea of sponsoring a different military member each month. In English class the children can write letters; in art class they can draw pictures; in Sunday school they can put together care packages. A child's experiences with a caring community can teach lessons in altruism and create an *others* orientation that will last a lifetime.

Be sure to get instructions for shipment before sending care packages so all regulations are followed. Care package options might include:

Toiletry Pack—Sample-size shaving cream, disposable razors, wet wipes, deodorant, toothpaste, toothbrush, floss, swabs, shampoo, lotion, bug repellent, foot powder, and socks.

Food Pack—Presweetened drink mix, jerky, granola bars, power bars, candy (nonchocolate), gum, canned soup, canned fruit, fruit snacks, nuts, and trail mix.

Smart Pack—Books of all kinds, a modern translation Bible, crossword puzzles, stationery, stamps, phone cards, online gift certificates, and fact books.

"I just want to thank all the people and organizations that support us. The response has been encouraging and welcome. Sometimes all it takes is a simple 'thank you' or 'we care' to make it through the next day." SSG "Nova" Army, Copperas Cove, Texas

Twenty Free Gifts You Can Sow into Lives

I'd like to end this book with gifts of tremendous, even eternal, value that are given at no cost to the giver. These are gifts any family member can give at any time. As you seek to live on one income, don't forget to make a difference in the lives of others and train your children to do the same.

1. Fix broken fences by mending a quarrel.
2. Seek out friend you haven't seen in a while.
3. Hug someone and whisper, "I love you."
4. Forgive an enemy and pray for him.
5. Be patient with an angry person.
6. Express gratitude to someone.
7. Make a child smile.
8. Find the time to keep a promise.
9. Make or bake something for someone—anonymously.
10. Speak kindly to a stranger and tell him a joke.
11. Enter another's sorrows and cut the pain in half.
12. Smile. Laugh a little. Laugh a lot.

13. Take a walk with a friend.

14. Kneel down and pat a dog.

15. Lessen your expectations of others.

16. Apologize if you were wrong.

17. Turn off the TV and talk.

18. Pray for someone who helped you when you hurt.

19. Give a soft answer even though you feel strongly.

20. Make friends with someone with whom you have nothing in common—and everything.

NOTES

Chapter 1: Mommy's Gone Wild

1. Robert Bernstein, "'Stay-at-Home' Parents Top 5 Million, Census Bureau Reports" November 30, 2004, www.census.gov.

2. Beth Brykman, *The Wall Between Women: The Conflict Between Stay-at-home and Employed Mothers* (Amherst, NY: Prometheus Books, 2006), 58.

Chapter 2: I Can't Afford to Stay Home

1. M. P. Dunleavey, "Cost of Being a Stay-at-Home Mom: $1 Million," www.moneycentral.msn.com.

2. Arlie Hochschild, *The Second Shift* (New York: Penguin, reissue 2003), 182.

3. Dan Malachowski, "Report on How Much Stay-At-Home Moms Would Earn," www.salary.com, May 6, 2005.

4. Ibid.

5. Daniel Akst, "Second Incomes: Twice the Work, Half the Return," www.moneycentral.msn.com, January 2006.

6. Linda Kelley, *Two Incomes and Still Broke?* (New York: Times Books, 1996), 135.

Chapter 4: The Family Meeting

1. Stephen Covey, *The Seven Habits of Highly Effective People* (New York: Free Press, 2004), 189.

Chapter 6: Three, Four, or More

1. Age Venture News Service, "Millennium Manifests Gen-X Moral Majority," www.demko.com, Generation 2001 Study from Northwestern Mutual, April 5, 2006.

Chapter 8: The Wednesday Factor

1. Peter Greenberg, Fodors Travel Wire, "Best Day to Buy Cheap Tix," www.fodors.com, April 2005.
2. Steve Hargreaves, "The Best Time to Buy Everything," www.CNNMoney.com, January 2006.

Chapter 9: Taming the 800-Pound Gorilla

1. Liz Pullian Weston, "Beef Up Your Credit Score in Five Steps," www.moneycentral.msn.com, August 2006.
2. Ibid.
3. Ibid.
4. Jean Chatzky, "Smart Home Projects," (*USA Weekend*, April 2006), 6.
5. Ibid.
6. Federal Trade Commission. "Home Sweet Home Improvement," (*FTC Facts for Consumers*), 2–3.
7. Walecia Konrad, "MoneySmart," (*USA Weekend*, January 15, 2006), 15.

Chapter 10: That's *My* Business

1. Ann Crittenden, *The Price of Motherhood: Why the Most Important Job in the World Is Still the Least Valued* (New York: Owl Books, 2002), 78.
2. Donna Partow, *Homemade Business* (Colorado Springs: Focus on the Family, 1992), 123.
3. Priscilla Y. Huff, "Start Making Money at Home," www.DrLaura.com, Info. Guide #G37.
4. Bernard C. Kamoroff, *Small Time Operator* (Willits, CA: Bell Springs, 2006), 14.
5. Jane Pollack, *Soul Proprietor: 100 Lessons from a Lifestyle Entrepreneur* (New York: Crossings Press, 2001), 74.

Moody Publishers is the Name Women Trust

for growth inward, outward, and upward.

MOODY
PUBLISHERS

Find these and other women's titles at your favorite bookstore or online.

To Contact Ellie Kay:

Ellie Kay and Company, LLC
3053 Rancho Vista Blvd, Suite H-102
Palmdale, CA   93551
(661) 547-6820

www.elliekay.com

*Come visit
our website
for coupons,
a newsletter
for the
latest saving
tips, and to
see if Ellie is in
your neighborhood!*

www.EllieKay.com

Things I need to remember

Price Living

Secrets to Living Well on One Income

ELLIE KAY
AMERICA'S FAMILY FINANCIAL EXPERT

Things I need to remember